Carving Down-Home Angels with Tom Wolfe

Tom Wolfe

Schiffer® Publishing Ltd

4880 Lower Valley Road, Atglen, PA 19310 USA

Library of Congress Control Number: 2005928643

Designed by Joseph M. Riggio Jr.
Type set in Zurich BT

ISBN: 0-7643-2326-1
Printed in China

Published by Schiffer Publishing Ltd.
4880 Lower Valley Road
Atglen, PA 19310
Phone: (610) 593-1777; Fax: (610) 593-2002
E-mail: Info@schifferbooks.com

For the largest selection of fine reference books on this and related subjects, please visit our web site at **www.schifferbooks.com**
We are always looking for people to write books on new and related subjects. If you have an idea for a book please contact us at the above address.

This book may be purchased from the publisher.
Include $3.95 for shipping.
Please try your bookstore first.
You may write for a free catalog.

In Europe, Schiffer books are distributed by
Bushwood Books
6 Marksbury Ave.
Kew Gardens
Surrey TW9 4JF England
Phone: 44 (0) 20 8392-8585; Fax: 44 (0) 20 8392-9876
E-mail: info@bushwoodbooks.co.uk
Free postage in the U.K., Europe; air mail at cost.

Introduction

I guess my mind runs a bit off the beaten path, but when I think of angels what I see are not the glowing, finely dressed perfect beings like most people seem to think. An ol' preacher once told me that angels are nothing more than messengers from God. That means they get down with us, meet us face to face, so they can give us an important message. I often think of Clarence in that great old movie "A Wonderful Life." He didn't appear in a flash of light or with a heavenly choir, but in an old wrinkled over coat and a rumpled fedora. That's how it is, I suspect. When God wants to tell us something he sends someone we would be comfortable with. So it is with these angels. A little wrinkled and a lot ugly, they are the real thing, and proof that God must have a sense of humor.

Of course, we country folk don't always see eye to eye with angels. I heard about four guys from West Virginia who died and went to heaven. When they arrived, St. Peter stopped them at the Pearly Gates.

"I don't know if I can let you guys in here," he challenged. Looking up their names in his great book he read out loud, "moonshining... chewing tobacco... womanizin'... Why you fellas ain't nothing but ne'er-no-goods."

The four men looked down at their feet, a bit ashamed, but not willing to give up. "That can't be the whole story. There must be something good about us in there. We ain't *that* bad."

Feeling a bit sorry for them, St. Peter offered to go up to the big house and talk to God. When he got there he opened up the book and read the sorry list of woes.

When he finished, God thought for a minute, then told St. Peter. "Those guys done things you don't know about...Why just last week Clem was speeding down the mountain and missed hitting old Mrs. Murphy by about half an inch. She was so happy to be alive that she fell on her knees and repented of her sins right there and then. I tell you, with the lives they've lived they made believers out of a whole lot of people! Go down there and let 'em in."

Happy for them but a little surprised, St. Peter left the big house and went back to the Pearly Gates. But it wasn't 20 seconds later when he was back in front of God, panting as if he had run the whole way, which of course he hadn't. "They're gone!" he shouted.

"You mean the gentlemen from West Virginia left?"

"No, the gates. They stole the Pearly Gates!"

• • • • •

The only other angel story I know involves Santa Claus, one of my favorite characters. One Christmas he was having a bad time. The elves were threatening to go on strike. Mrs. Claus was constantly after him about needing more quality time and why didn't he go on a diet and how about a December vacation in Florida? The reindeer it seemed had had enough of flying and wanted to mope around the barn. Old Santa was beside himself and beginning to wonder if this would be the year without Christmas. "I've just about had it with all of you!" he shouted at the top of his lungs to anyone within earshot.

Just then, a little angel came into the workshop dragging a Christmas tree behind her.

"What should I do with this tree, Santa?"

And that's why there's an angel on top of every Christmas tree.

Well, I hope this book brings you many years of enjoyment.

About Carving the Angels in this Book

The technique we are showing in this book does not rely on patterns, though we have included some for those who must have them.

It starts with a square block of wood. In this case it is as tall as it is square, but it can be any height. If the height is greater than the width, the angel will appear taller and skinnier, and will probably be standing.

By following the step-by-step instructions you can create a whole band of angels using the same techniques. Each one will be unique depending not only on the dimensions of the blank you use, but on the various features you give it.

Have fun!

Start with a block of basswood. It can be any size, just as long as it's square. This one is about 3 1/4" square and 7 1/2" long. This carving is going to be kneeling, so if you want a standing figure, use a taller block. First mark the block like this.

Then saw it with the bandsaw to look like this.

Use the piece you cut off to mark another line on the tall side.

Then cut on that line with the bandsaw, to get a piece that looks like this.

At the bottom of the curve, measure in and mark a spot 3/4 of an inch on each side. You can measure in further if you want, but remember, the farther in you measure, the thinner your angel will be.

Taper the lines toward the top so they come to the edge. The result should look like this.

Turn the block around and mark on the back corner for removal like this.

Cut the block on the bandsaw to look like this.

Again to the bandsaw for this result.

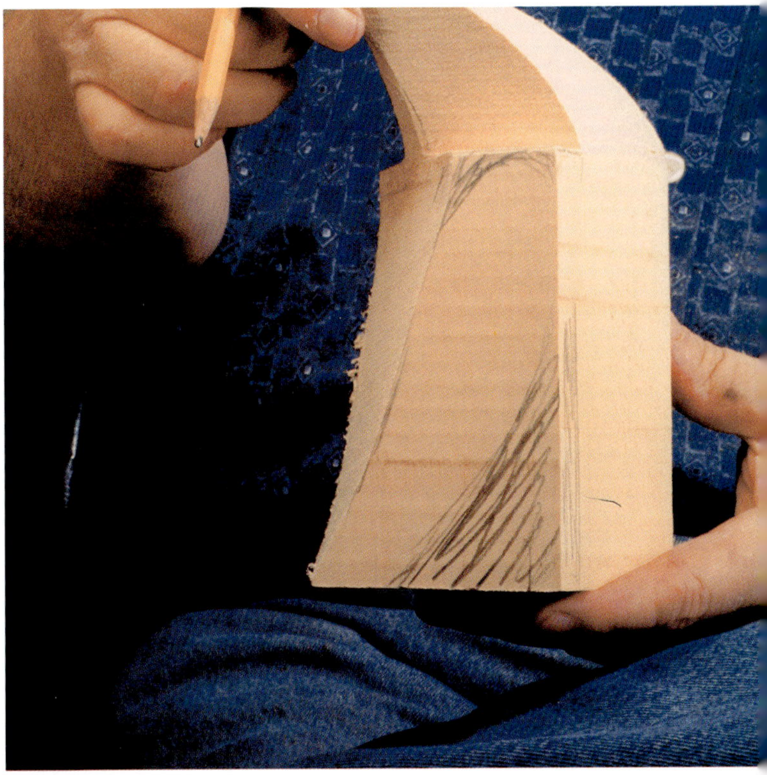

Now moving to the side, mark the curve of the lower and upper edge of the angel's wing. These areas can be carved out or, as I usually do, taken out with the drill press. The drill press is much quicker and easier on the hands.

For the last bit of preparation of the blank, we'll use the drill press. Measure in 1/2 inch on the outside edges of the front. Mark this for removal by darkening it.

The rough out is done and we are ready for carving.

I'll start carving by taking out some of the excess at the back of the shoulders to make room for the wings. Make a stop cut at the shoulder...

A helpful hint: To make carving easier, I've found that spraying the piece with a half-and-half solution of water and rubbing alcohol does the trick. The water allows for smoother carving and the alcohol helps it dry.

And cut back to it from the head. Keep making this kind of double cut until you've removed all the wood you want.

When the shoulders are defined, use a gouge to clean up the drill marks.

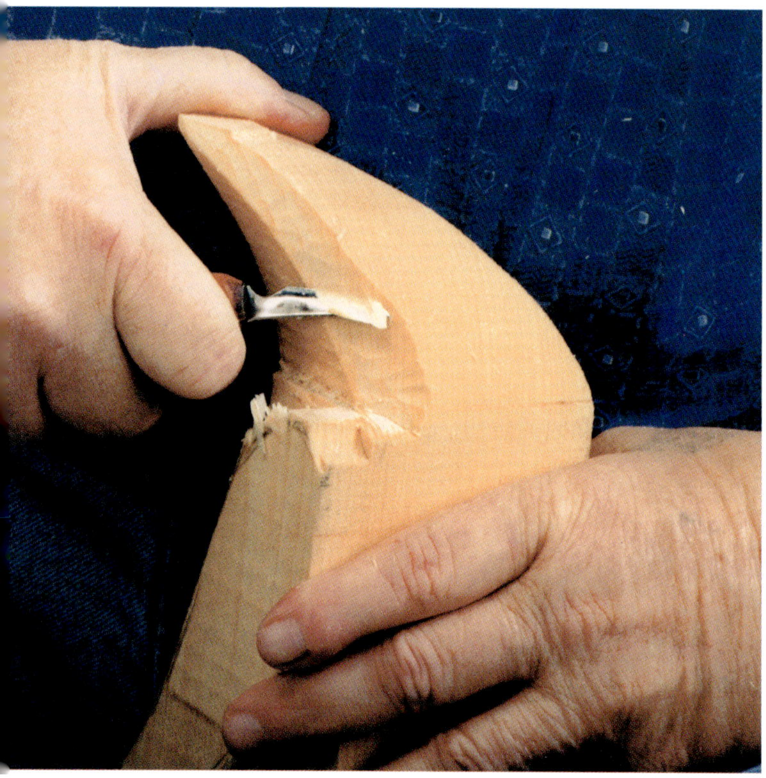

Continue to bring out the shoulder by reducing the head.

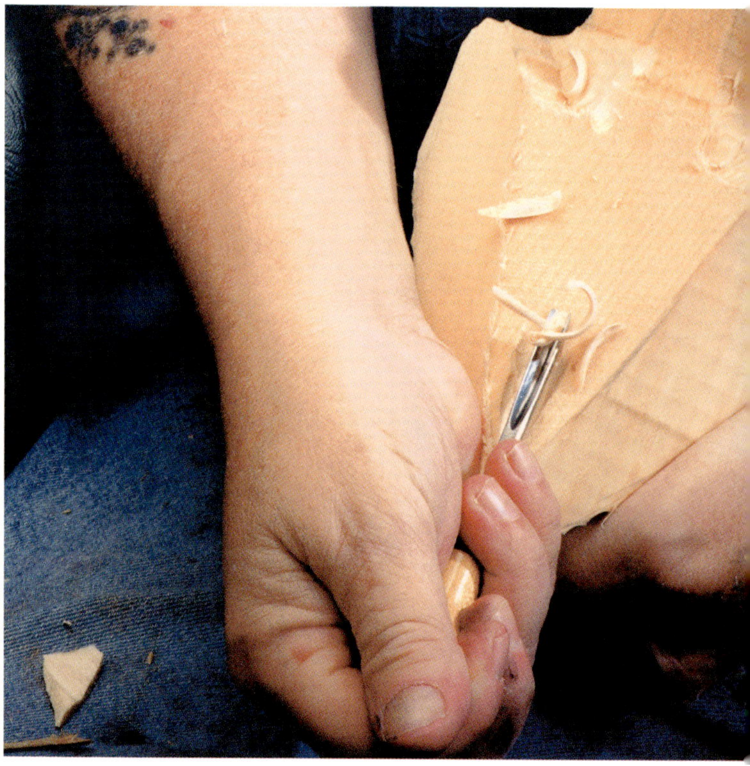

Turning the piece over, separate the wings by carving wood out between them.

Here you can see the progress on the head and wings from the back, as they take on their rough shape.

Moving to the front of the wing, Use a gouge between the head and the wing to define the top of the wing above the shoulder.

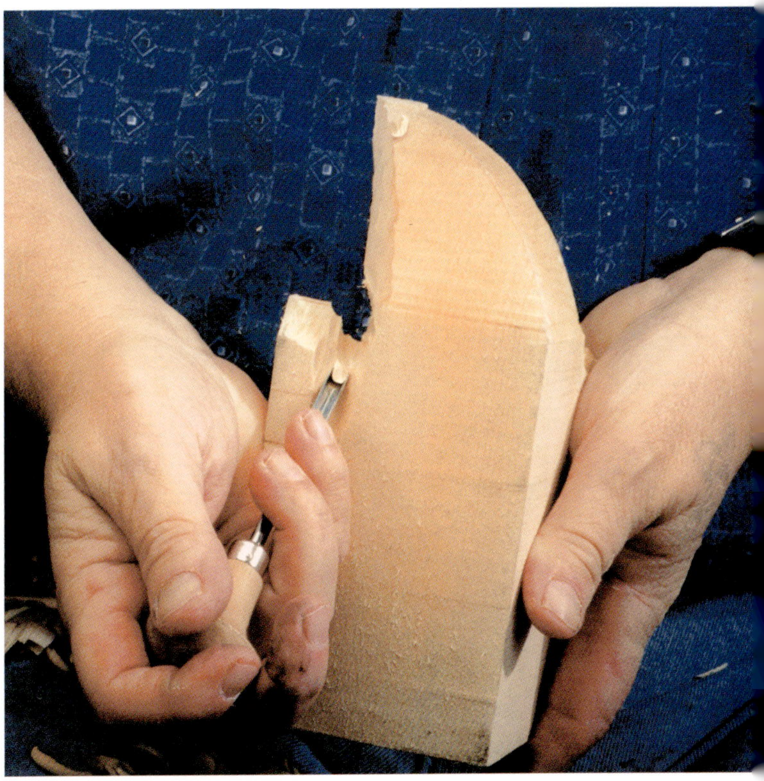

Continue to deepen the gulf.

The result.

Progress. Repeat on the other side.

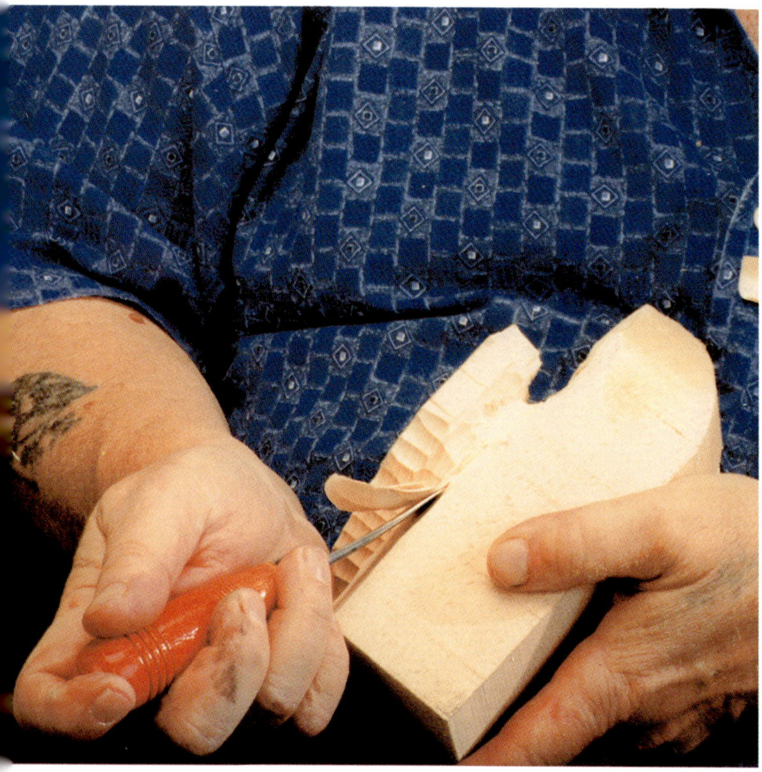

We need to carry the line of the body from the shoulder to the bottom of the piece. This will also bring out the leading edge of the wing. I do this with a gouge.

Cut back to the stop along the upper lip. This begins to bring the nose out from the face.

The bottom of the nose should be on a line with the top of the wings. Mark it and make a stop cut.

Next, use a scooping to cut to remove wood from the bridge of the nose.

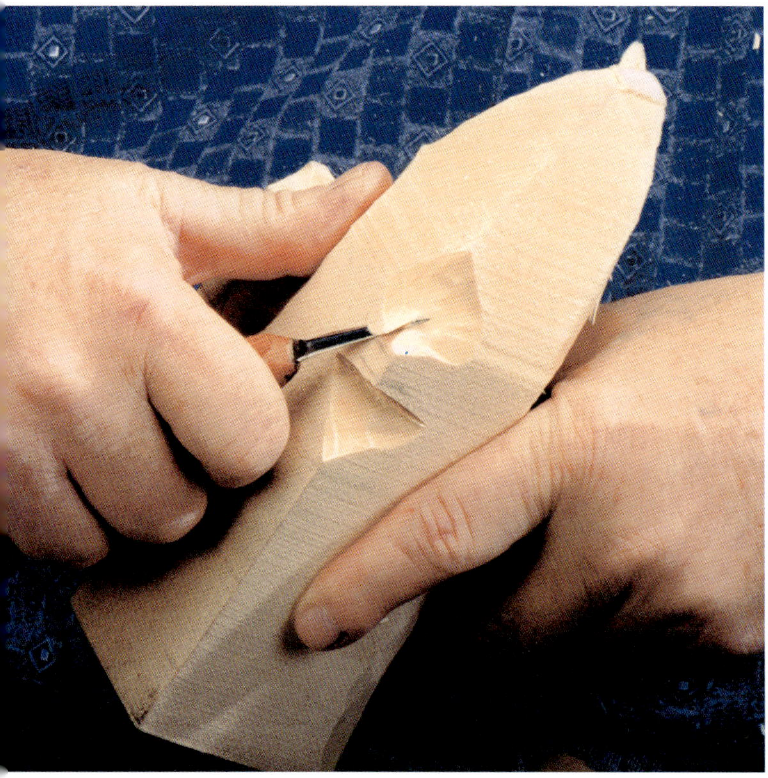

Carve away from the nose, leaving a large triangular shape fro the nose.

And trimming it off from the cheek.

Shape the lower corner of the nose by make a stop cut at an angle,

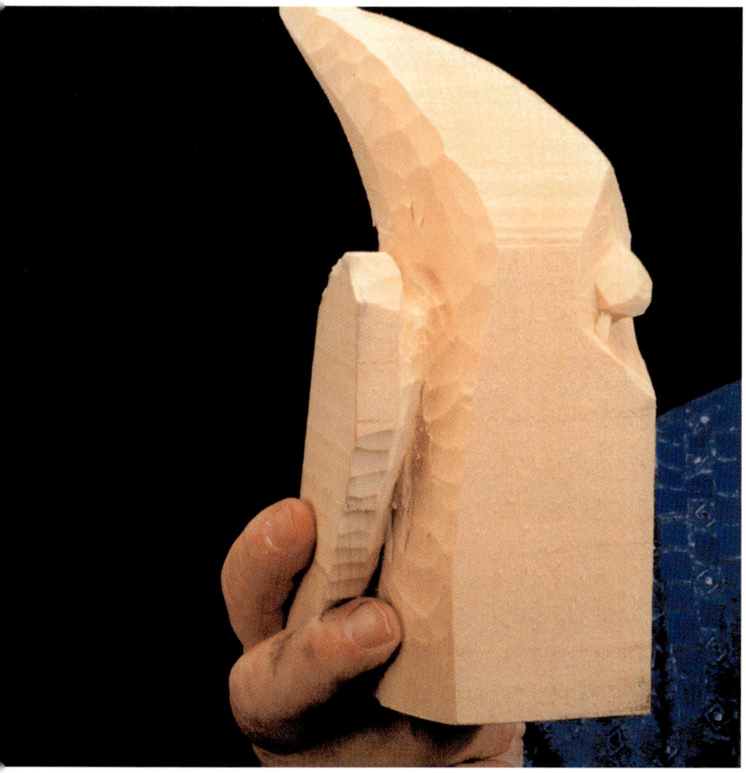

The profile is beginning to emerge. At this stage the area around the nose should be fairly flat.

Begin work on the beard by making a stop cut where the whiskers will end.

Before moving to the beard, I'm going to clean up the hat, rounding off the angular saw cuts left by the bandsaw.

When the bottom is defined, move to the side of the beard. Make a stop cut to set the shape.

Cut back to the stop from the chest. Repeat this process until the bottom of the beard reaches the depth you want.

Then cut back to it from the surface of the body. It is better to do this in a few smaller steps than to try to do it all in one deep cut. Repeat as necessary.

Here you can see the shape of the beard defined.

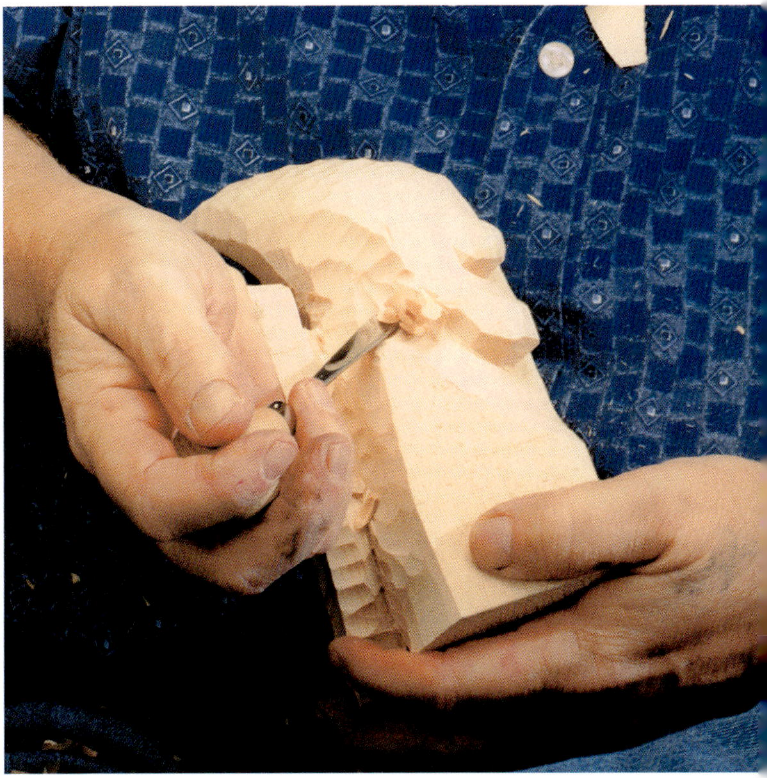

Use a gouge to shape the shoulder. I'm using a #7.

Draw a line to mark the top of the arm at the shoulder and repeat on the other side.

Cut a stop around the outline of the arm.

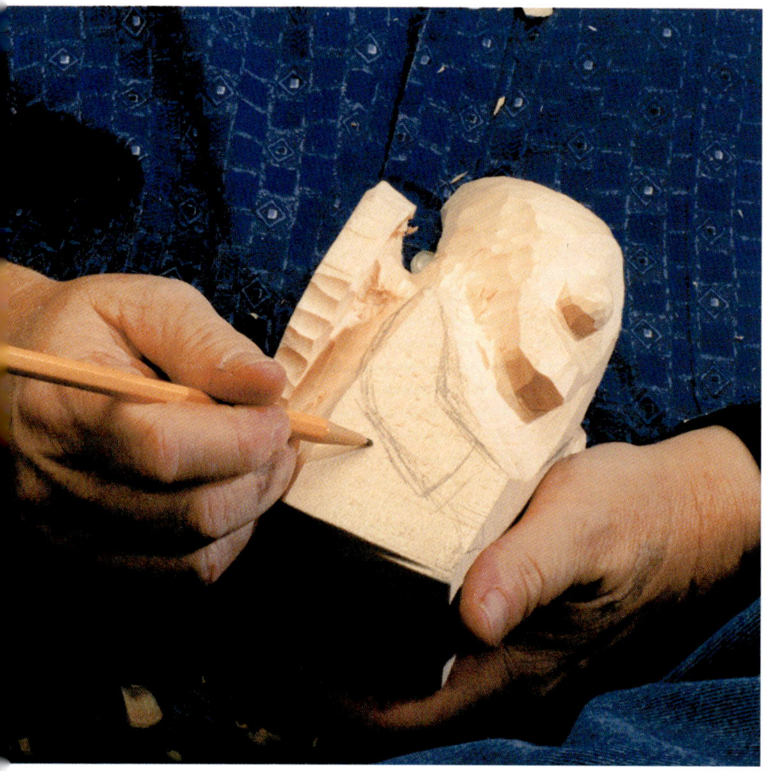

With the shoulder defined, we can mark the shape of the .

Trim back to the stop from the body to bring the arm out. Repeat as necessary, but temember to only go as deep as the thickness of the arms.

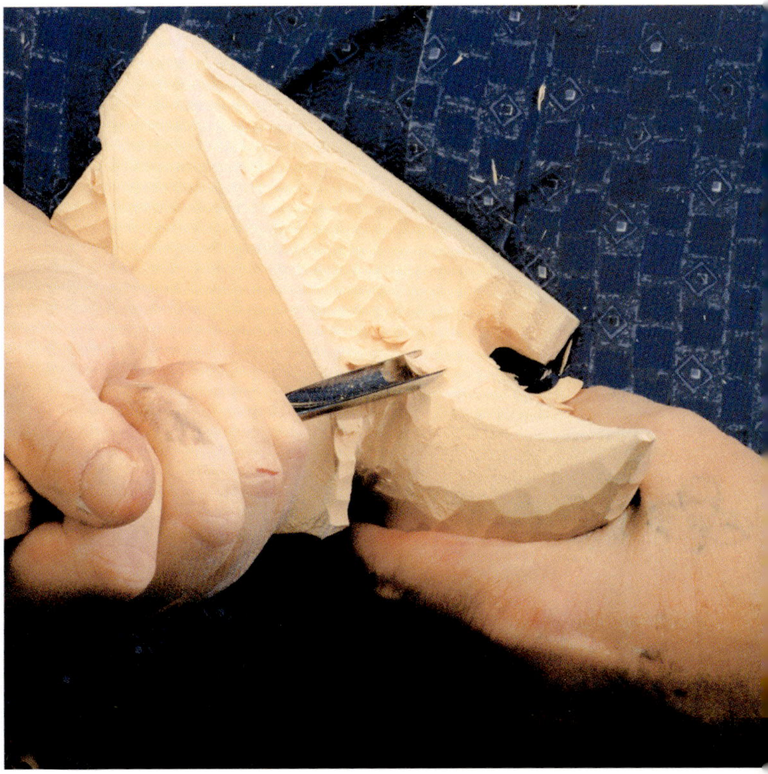

To fix this problem, remove more wood from the back of thes neck and all down his back.

Progress. The arms seem to be a little out of proportion.

It also helps to deepen the separation at the top of the wing so the butts of the wings come down behind the shoulders more.

Progress.

Next clean up the wings, rounding the surface and getting rid of some of those rough edges.

Returning to the front, we reduce the chest area a little bit, using a gouge.

I think I'll shorten that hat about an inch. As a character begins to take shape, it sometimes becomes clear that certain changes will make it look better. In this case it is simply a matter of popping the tip off like this...

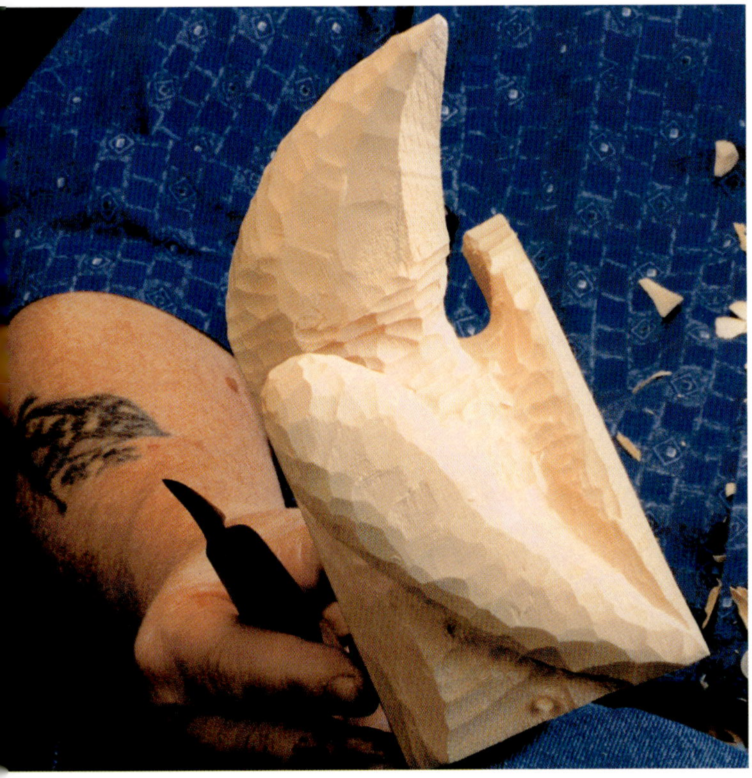

Progress.

and smoothing it back into a point.

I'm going to add a roll behind his neck where the fabric drapes. You can do this with a knife, cutting a stop from the top and trimming from the bottom.

We need to clear more wood out from between the wings. I'm using a V-tool here, where the wings come together.

Or you can use a v-gouge.

Now that everything is more proportional, attention can be paid to the details. A V-tool deepens the bottom line of the arm and acts as a stop cut.

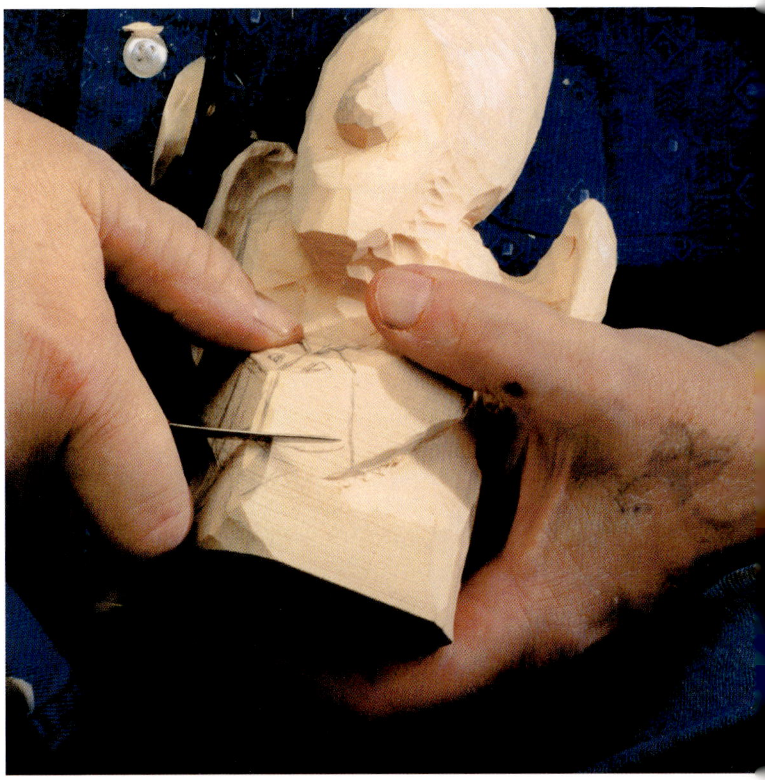

Make a stop cut under the hands.

Progress. With the shape of the arms established the hands can be drawn.

At the top of the hands make a stop cut on the line of each thumb

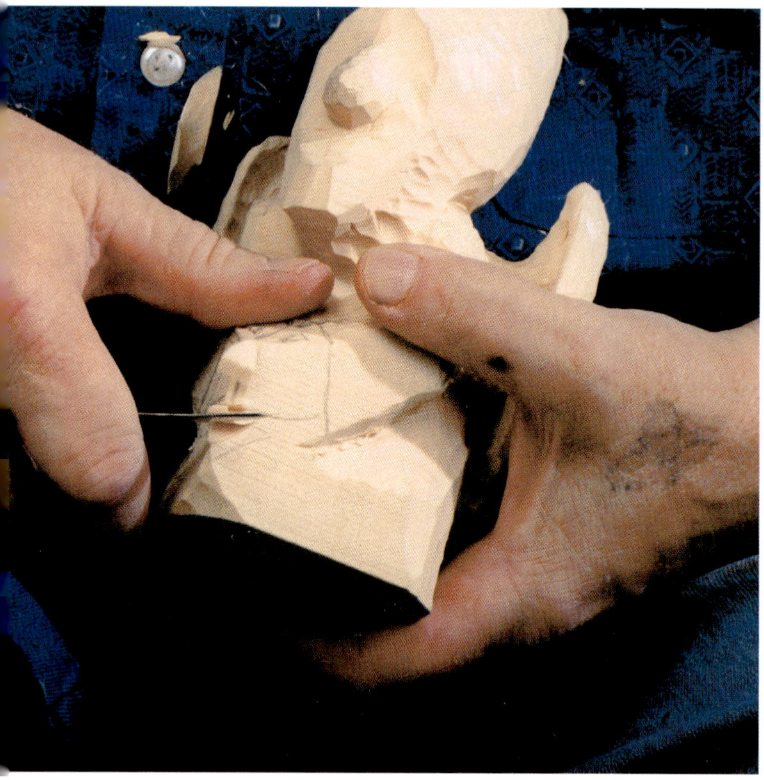

Trim back to the stop from the knees to define the lower line of the hands and bring them out from the body.

Make a third cut along the surface of the body. This creates a triangle that should pop right out and separate the wrists.

A small V-tool is used to separate the hands.

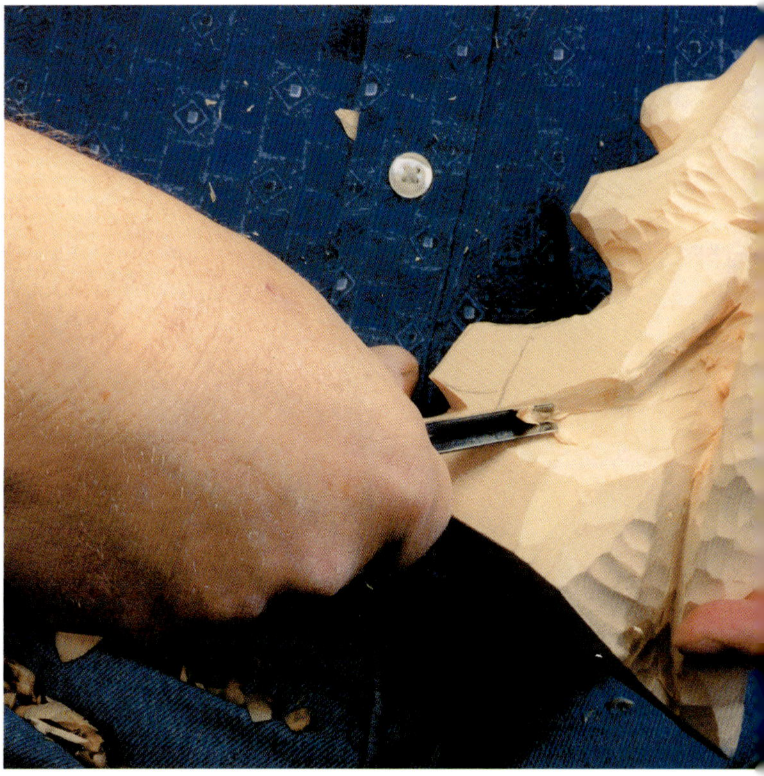

Carve the outside of the arm in the same way.

On the line between the arm and the chest, use a larger V-tool to deepen and define the separation, making them stand out more from body. This will also help to shape the arms.

To establish the sleeve, make a stop cut where the sleeve ends...

Trim back to it from the hand.

Progress.

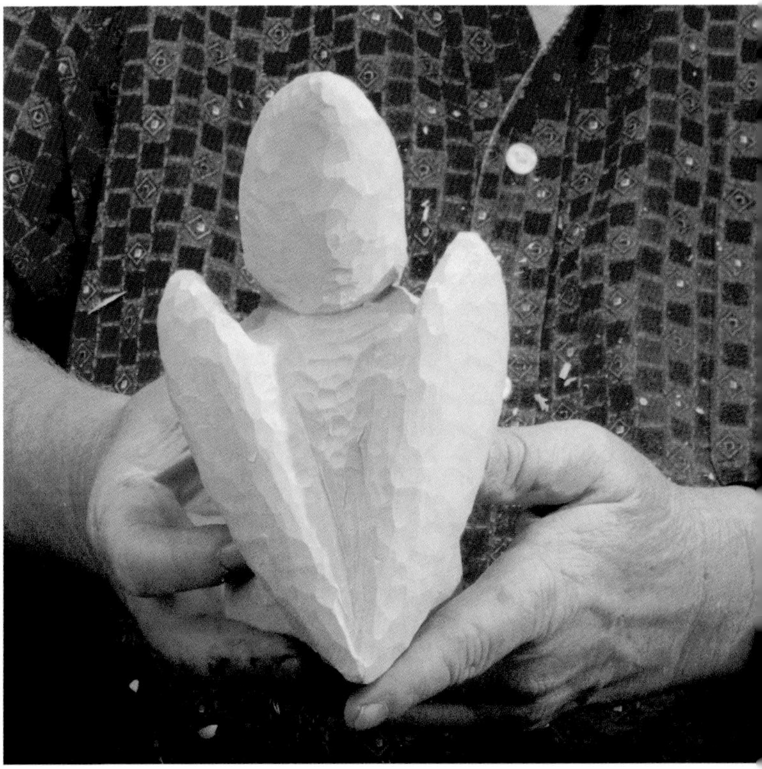

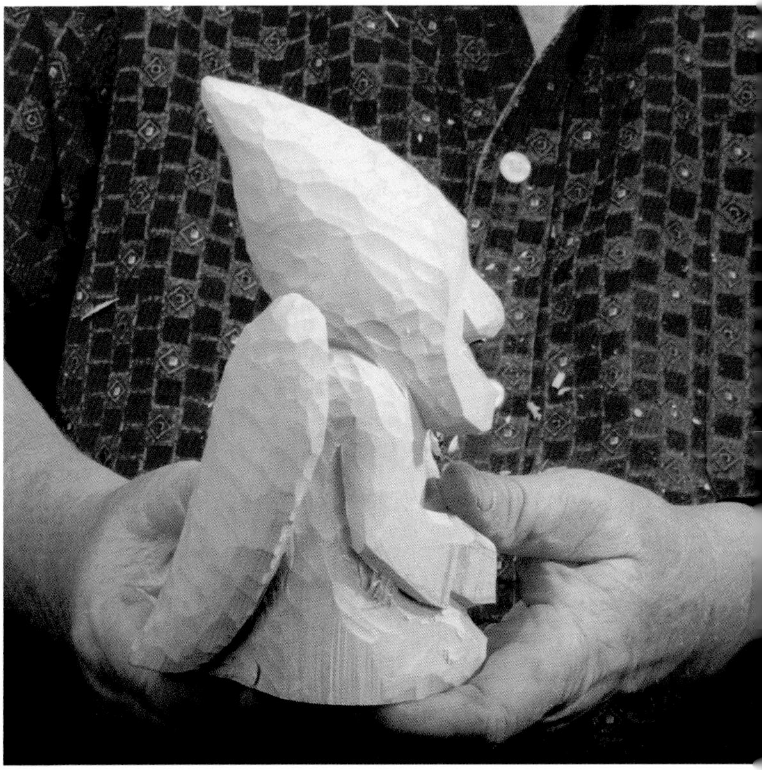

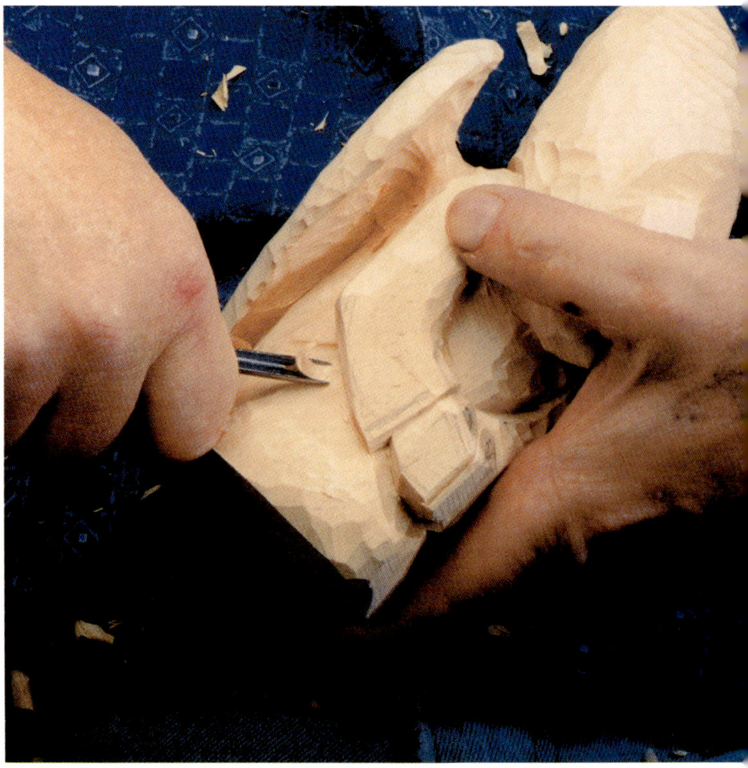

Using a small gouge, carve the folds in the fabric so they flow towards the waist.

The angel is kneeling, which creates some draping effect in the robe. Begin carving this by smoothing the leg area.

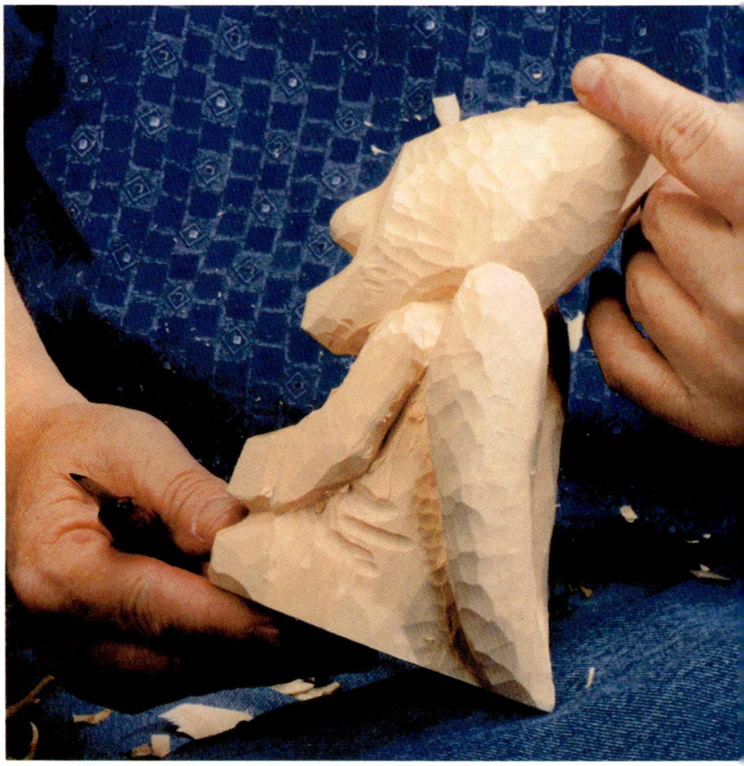

This is the result. Now he looks like he's kneeling.

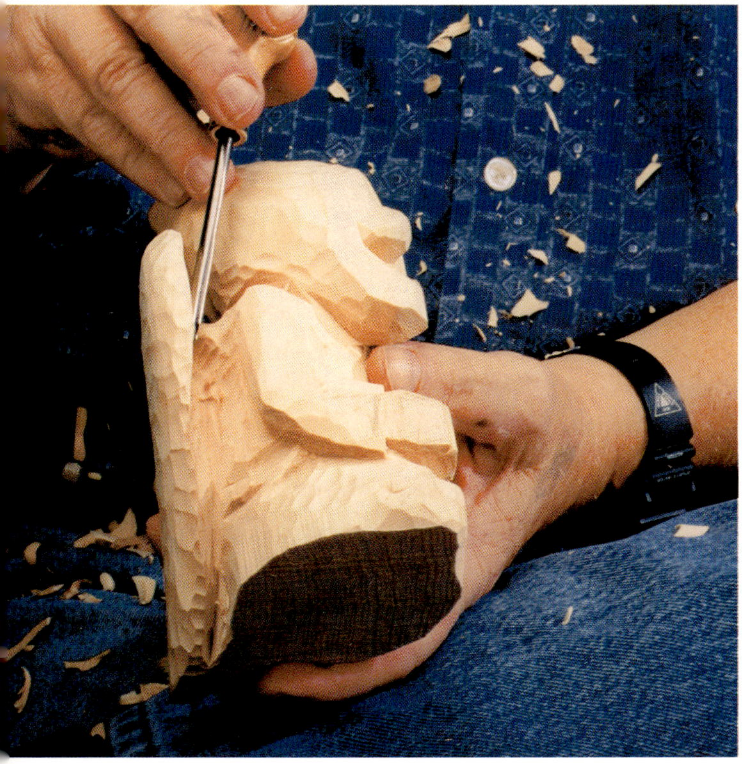

At this stage the wing is too heavy and not cupped enough.

With a gouge, carefully scoop the inner surface of the wing, moving from the outside edge toward the body. The goal is to make the wing thinner and more curved.

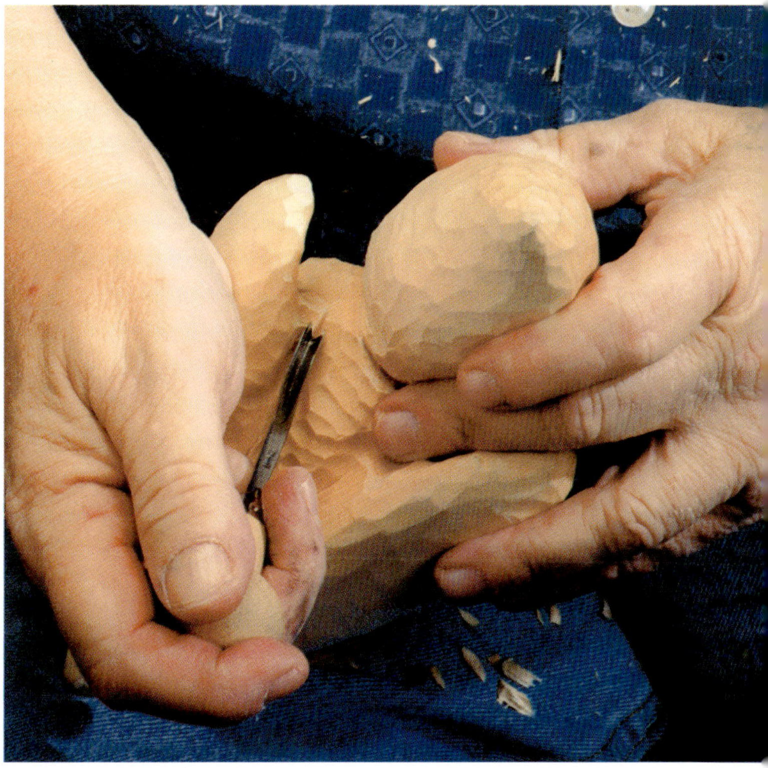

The wings are protruding from the angel's cloak, so I am going in with the V-tool to define the line where the fabric ends and the wing begins.

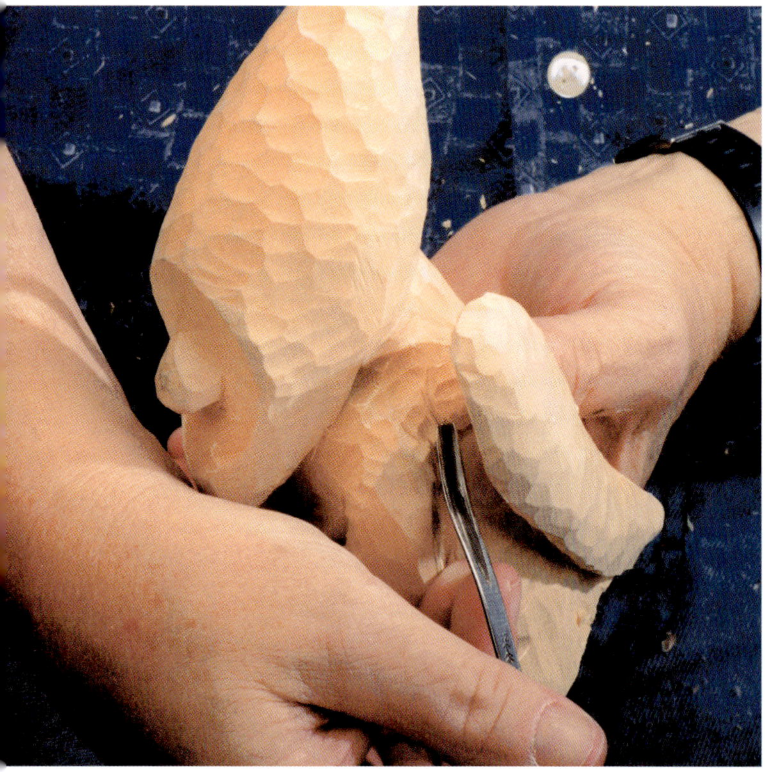

Continue the line around to the front.

The result. Mark the opening of the cloak and the edge of the hood around the face.

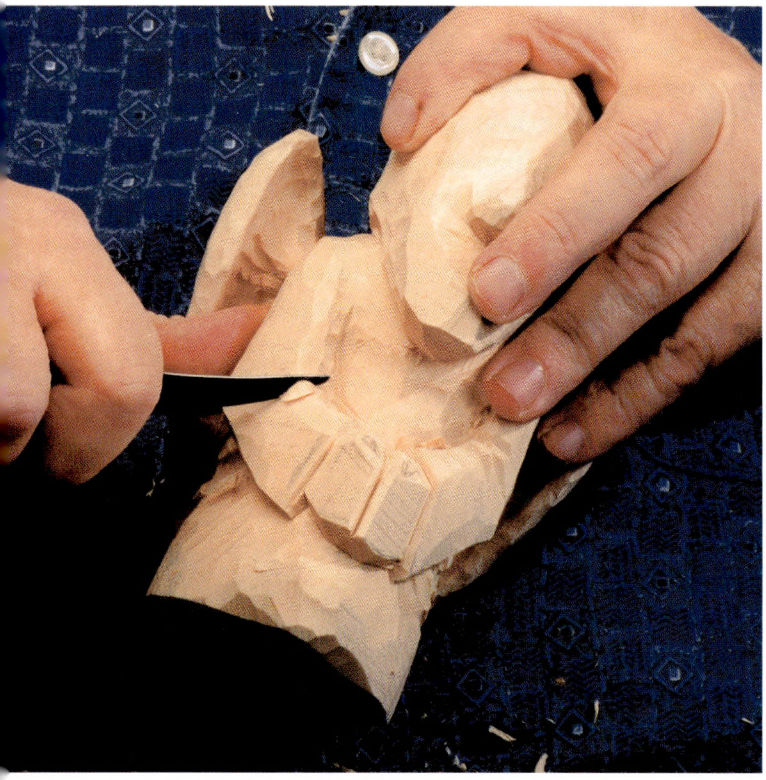

Three double-cuts make a crow's foot pattern in the crook of the arm.

Follow the lines of the robe and hood with the V-tool.

Trim back to the V-cuts from the face and body. This defines the cloak and its hood

Progress.

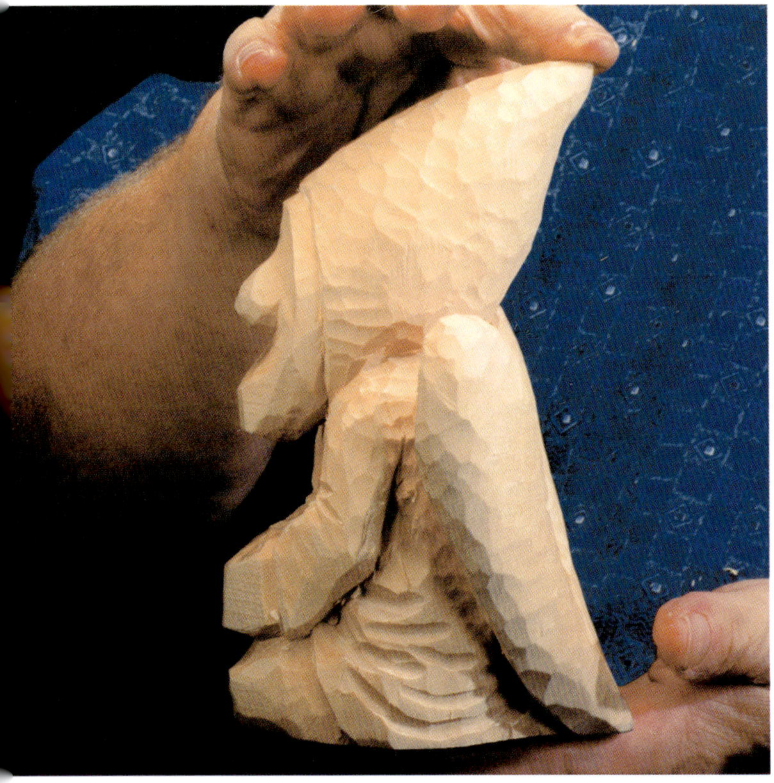

Now let's do some work on the face. Start by shaping the nose to make it symmetrical.

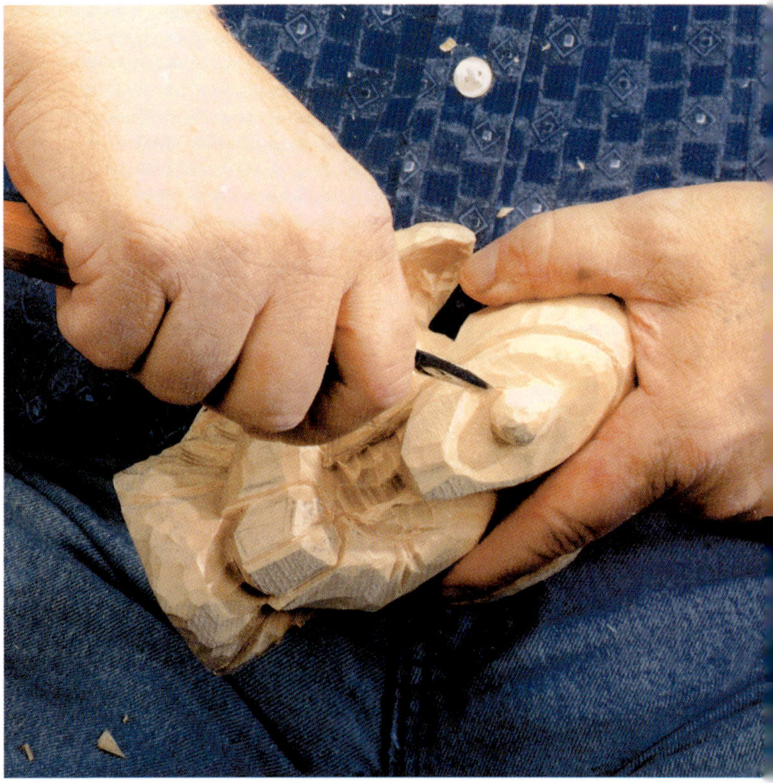

Next make a cut along the lower surface of the cheek, starting at the nose.

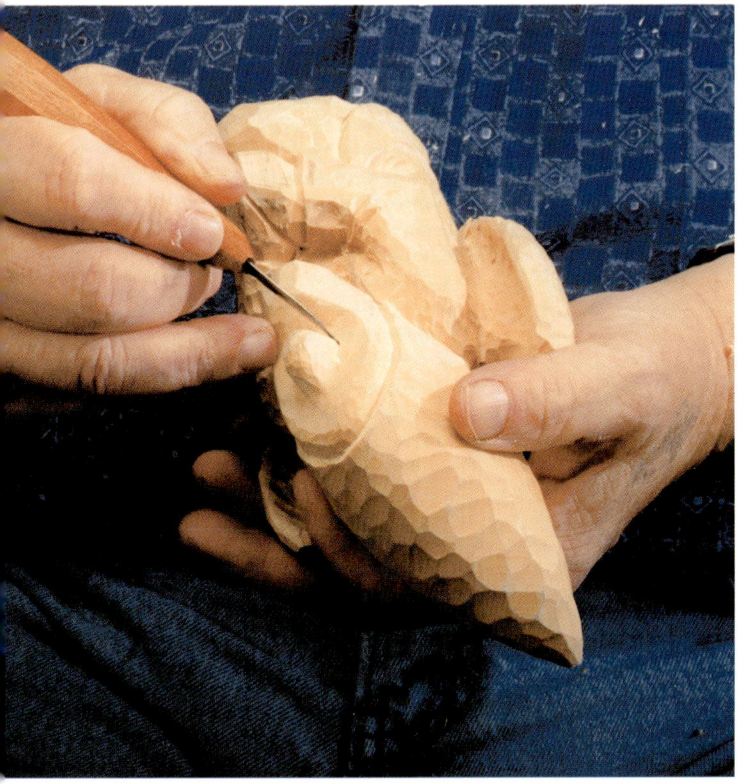

The smile line at the cheek beside the nose is created with three cuts. First make a stop along the side of the nose.

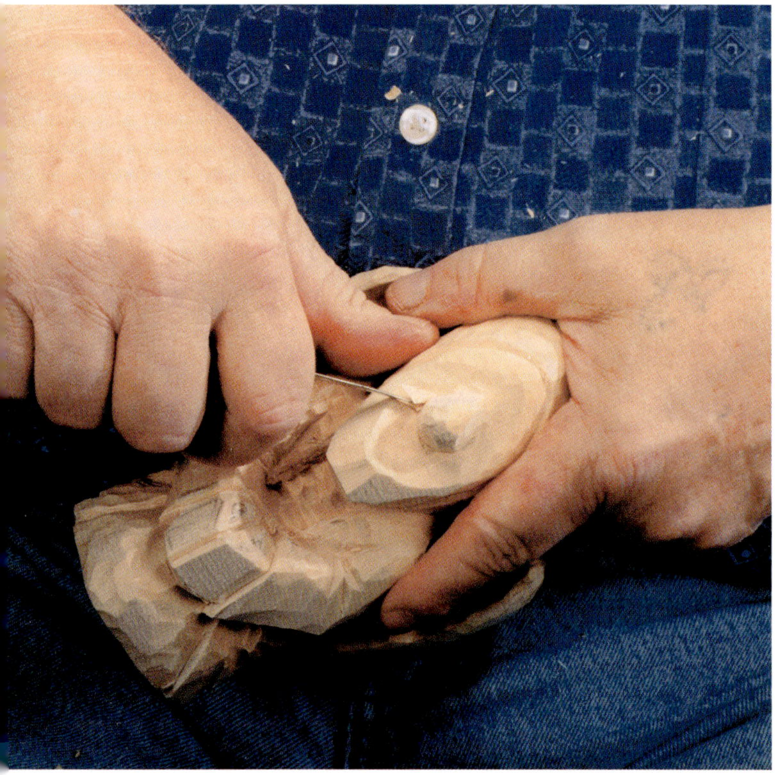

Finally make a cut from the surface of the lip, popping out the triangle this creates. Do this on each side of the nose.

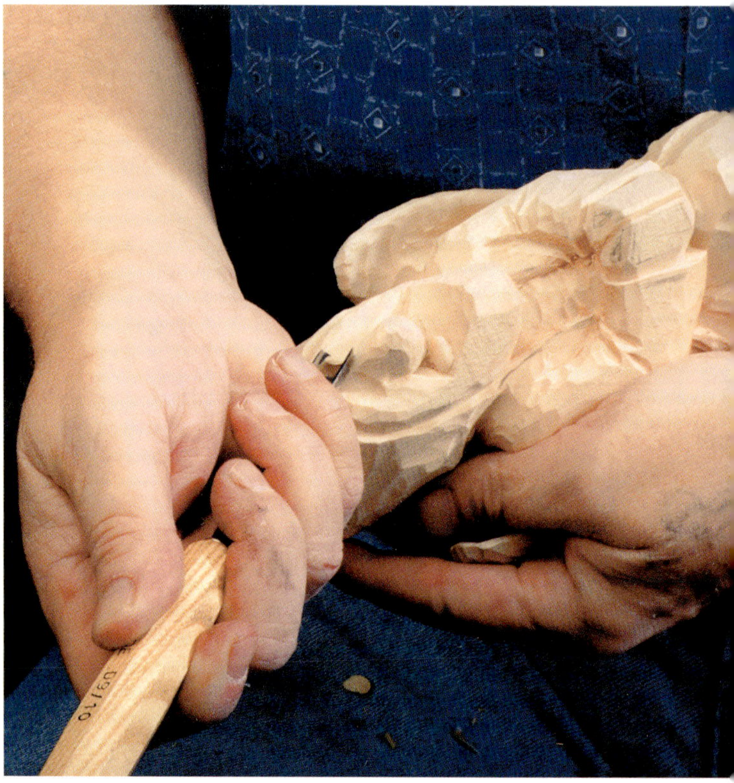

Using a half round gouge, work from the nose to the temple and remove wood from the eye areas.

Progress.

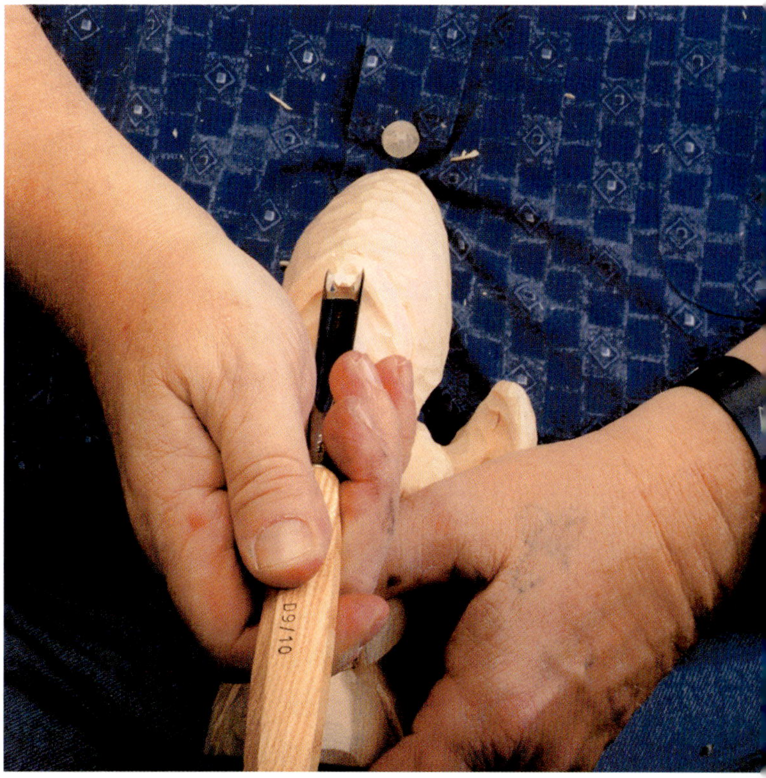

At the top of the nose, use a gouge separate the eyebrows.

Progress. The downward shape of the eye area gives him a mournful look.

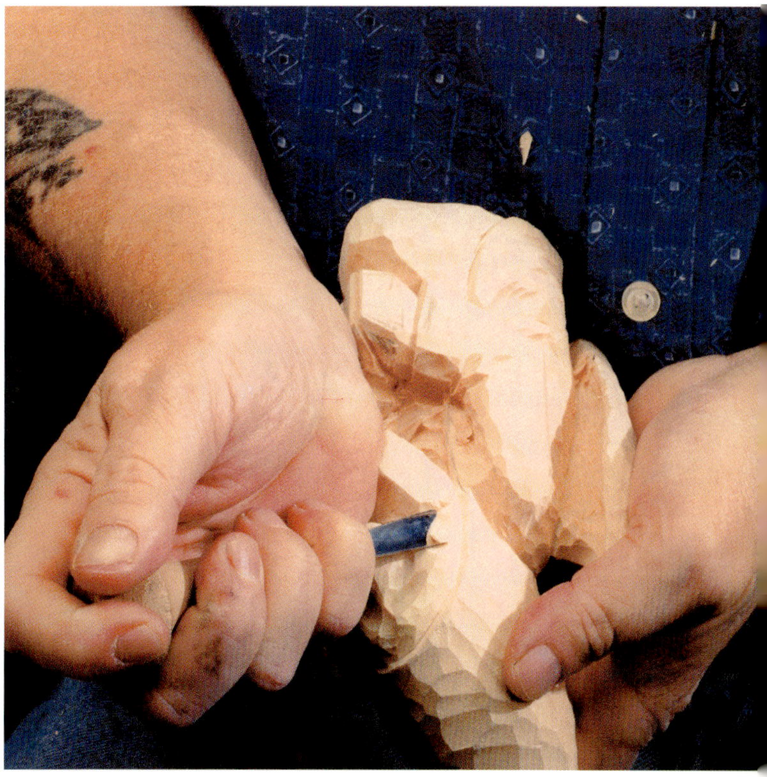

I want him to have more of a hollow-cheeked look, so I'm scooping wood out from under the cheekbones. Work from the front toward the back.

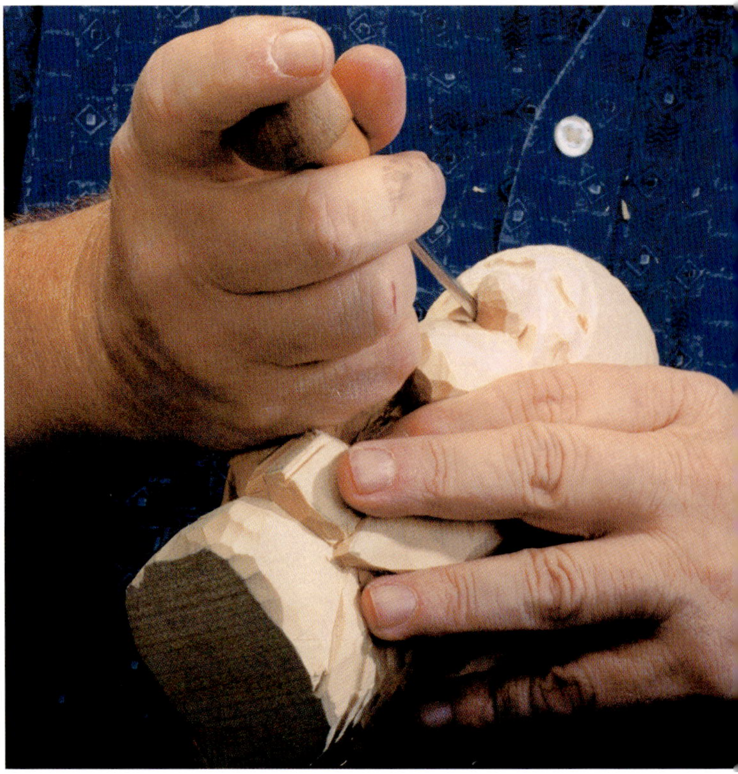

The same half round is good for making the nostrils; just push it right in, carrying the cut back to the lip.

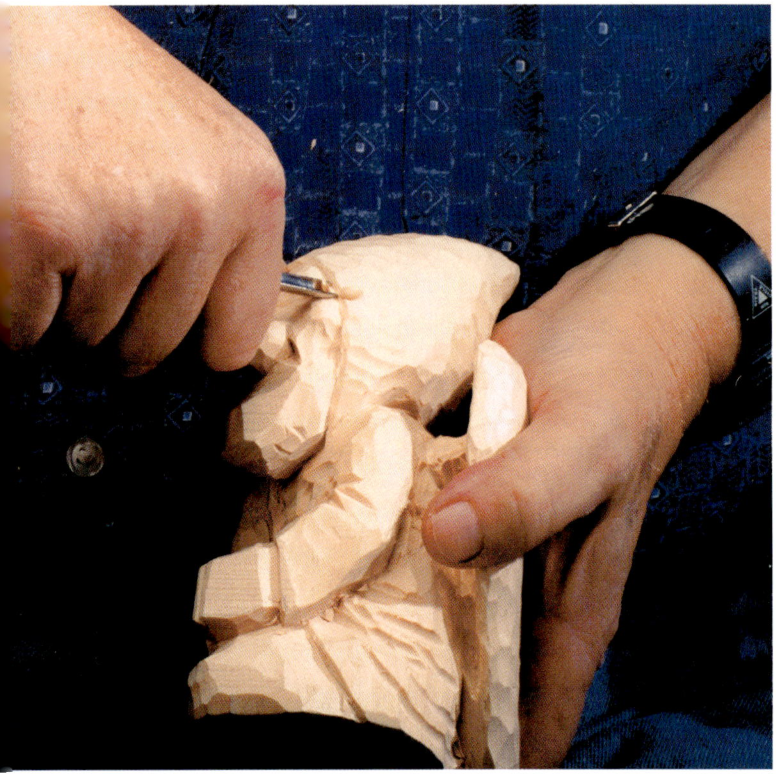

Using a small half round, carry the eye area back to the temple.

To create the outside flare of the nostril, start with the gouge at the tip of the nose and cut in an arc back to the face.

For the mouth, use the knife to make a 45-degree downward along the surface of the upper lip to the line where the lips will meet...

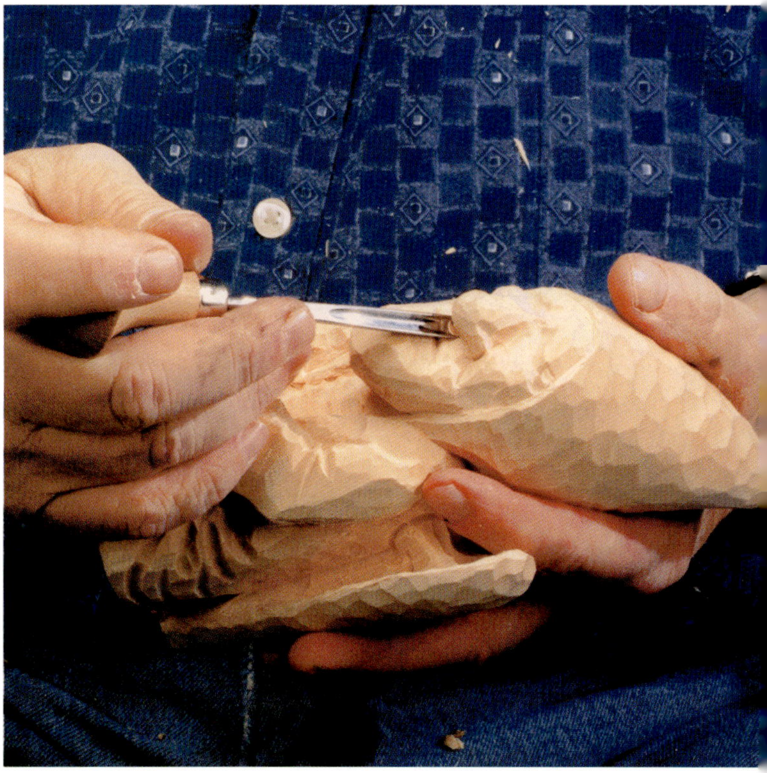

A little scoop with the half round gouge at the center of the upper lip creates the philtrum.

Come back to this line with another 45-degree slice along the surface of the lower lip.

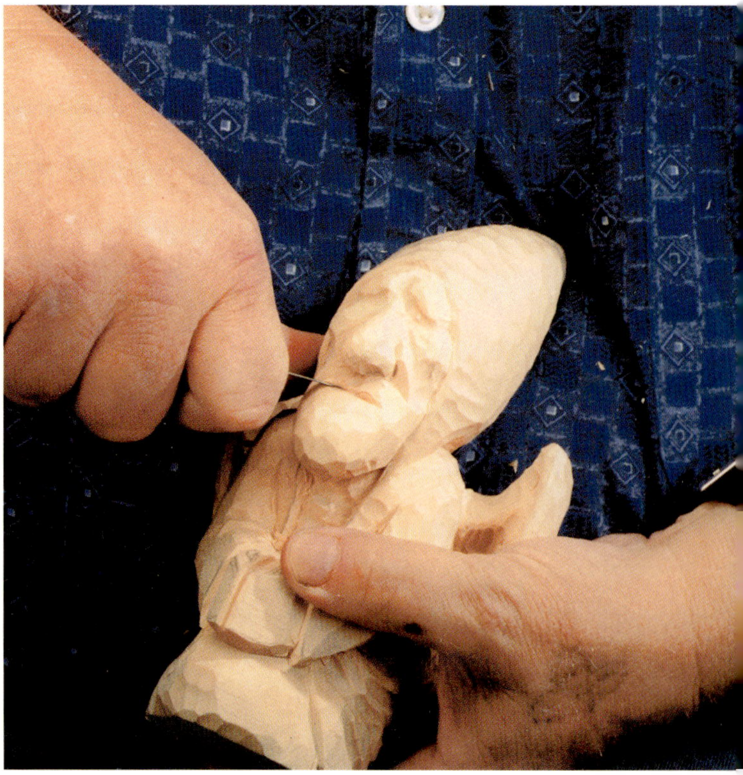

Then cut straight across to pop the piece out.

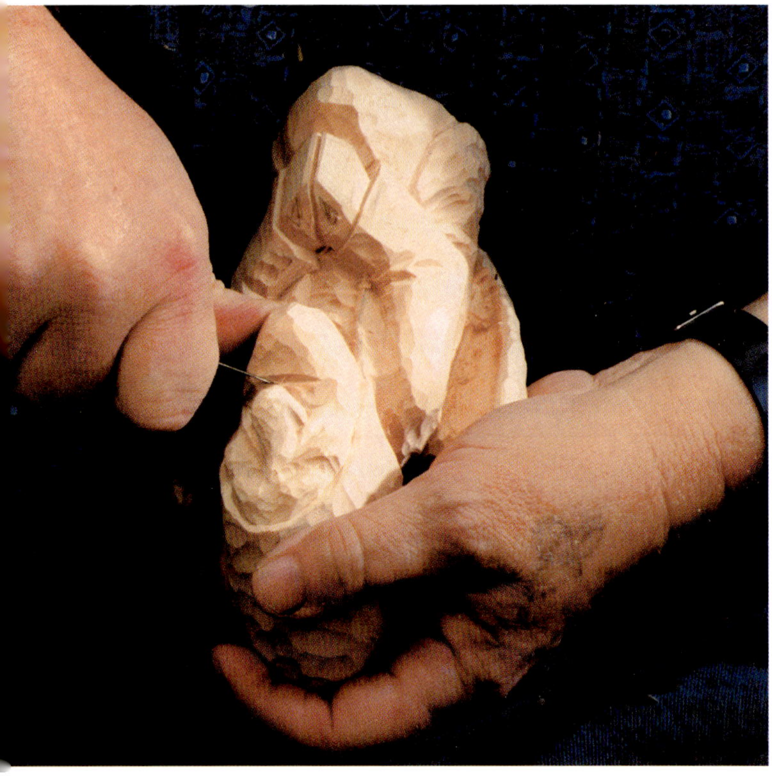

Starting at the center of the upper lip, pull the knife blade up, over, and down once in each direction. This shapes the upper lip.

Progress on the face.

The lower lip. He looks so unhappy!

Under the bottom lip, use the small half-round gouge to cut a groove, so the lip curls out naturally.

That can be fixed by turning up the corners of the mouth a little.

I can also scoop out the eye areas some more to raise the eyebrows.

Shape the nose to give him more of a button nose.

It might also help if the face wasn't so long. The beard can be trimmed to reduce the length of the face.

Progress on the face.

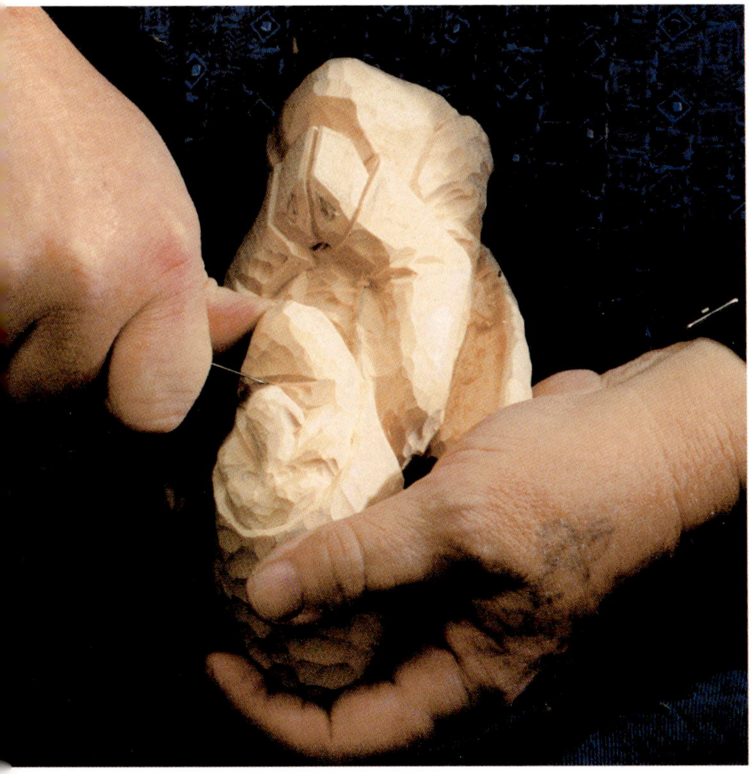

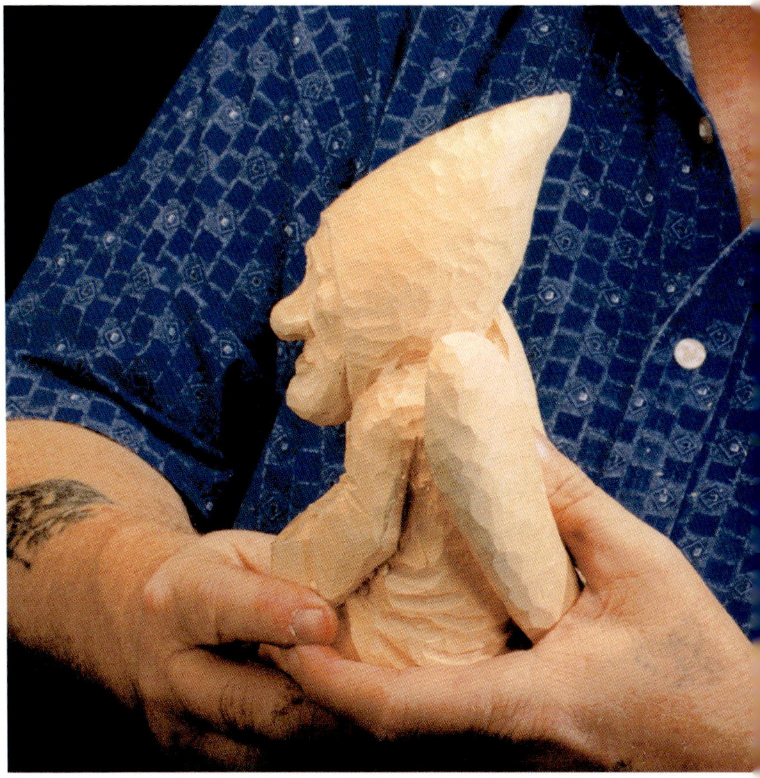

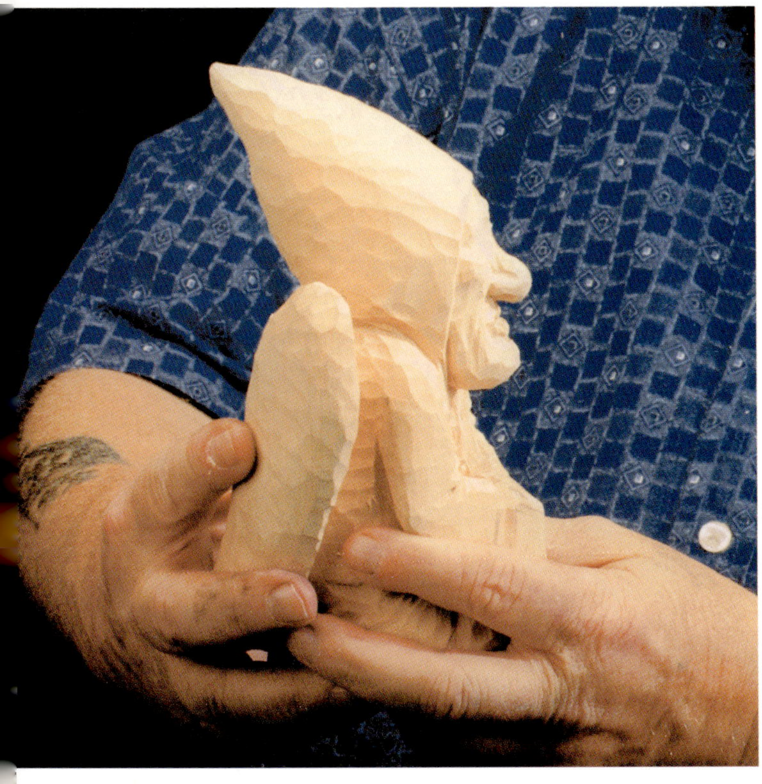

Now for the hands. To define thumbs we need to carve out the area between the thumb and forefinger. This is done with three cuts. First cut straight in along the line of the forefinger.

Finally come back from the V and lift up the wood between the thumb and forefinger.

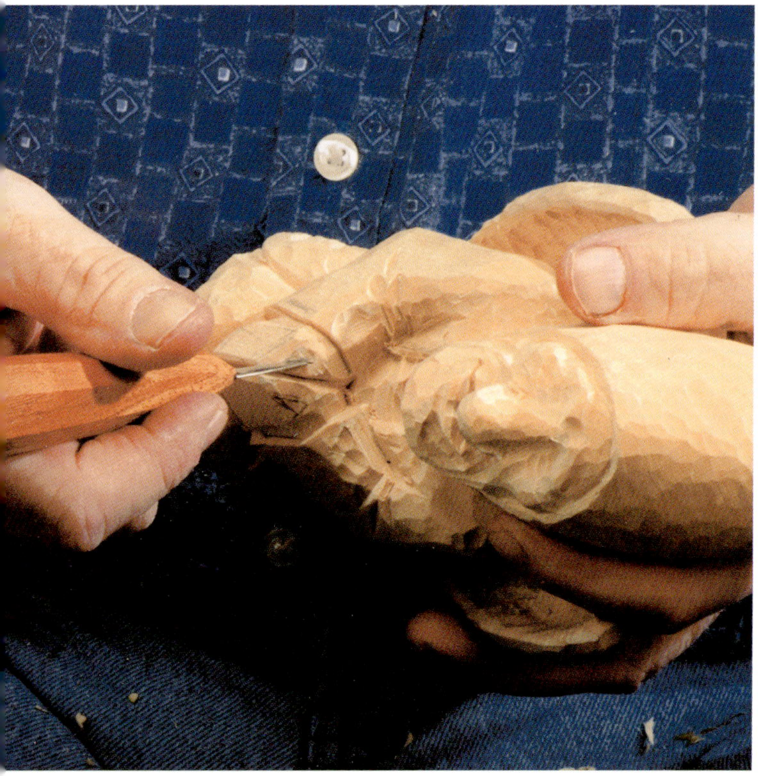

Then cut straight in along the line of the thumb.

Then lift make a third but from below to lift out the triangle.

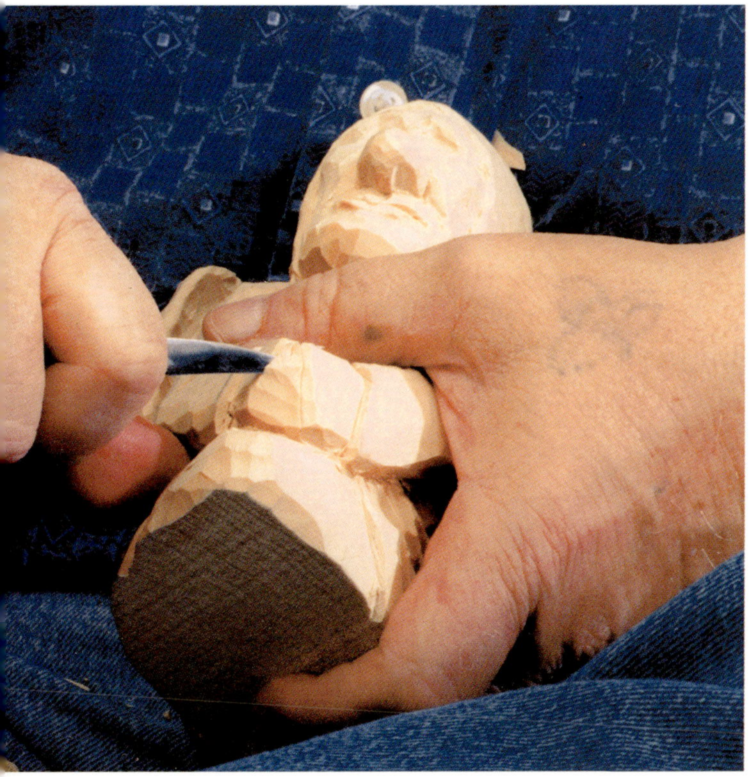

To open up the area where the hands meets, make a slicing cut down over the surface of the fingers.

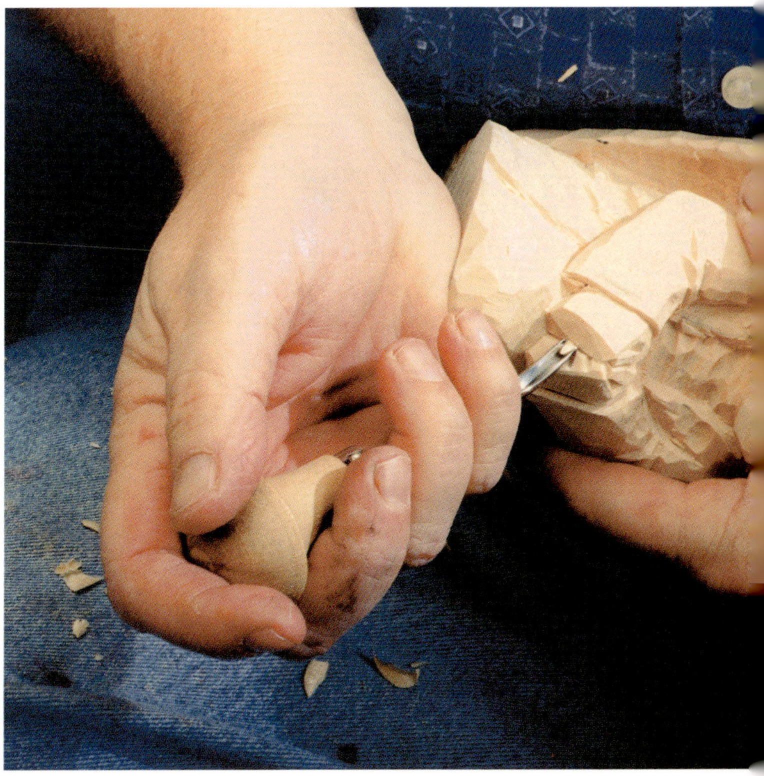

When this is done the fingers can be defined using a small V-tool to cut between them.

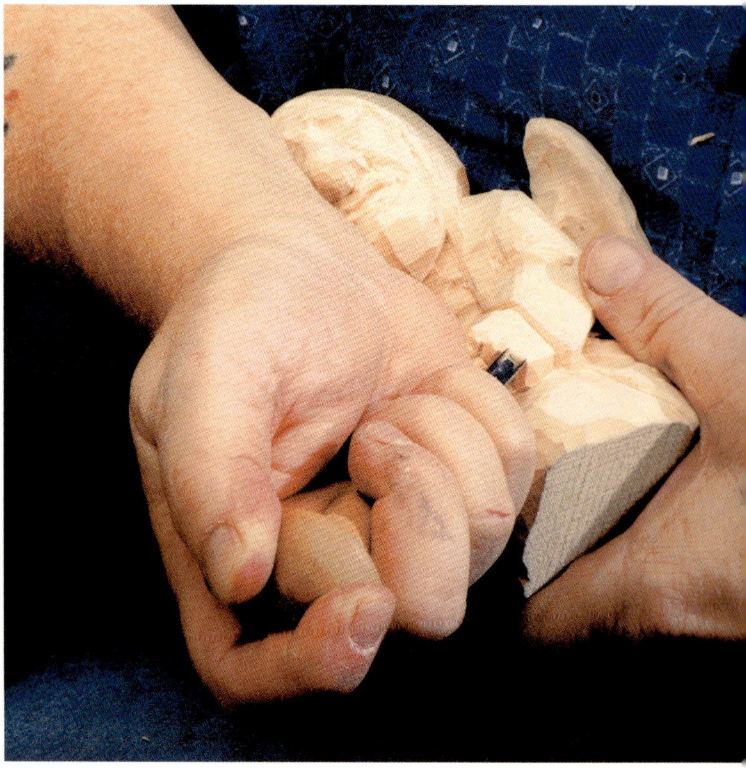

Using a gouge to take a little nip from between each V-cut creates knuckles.

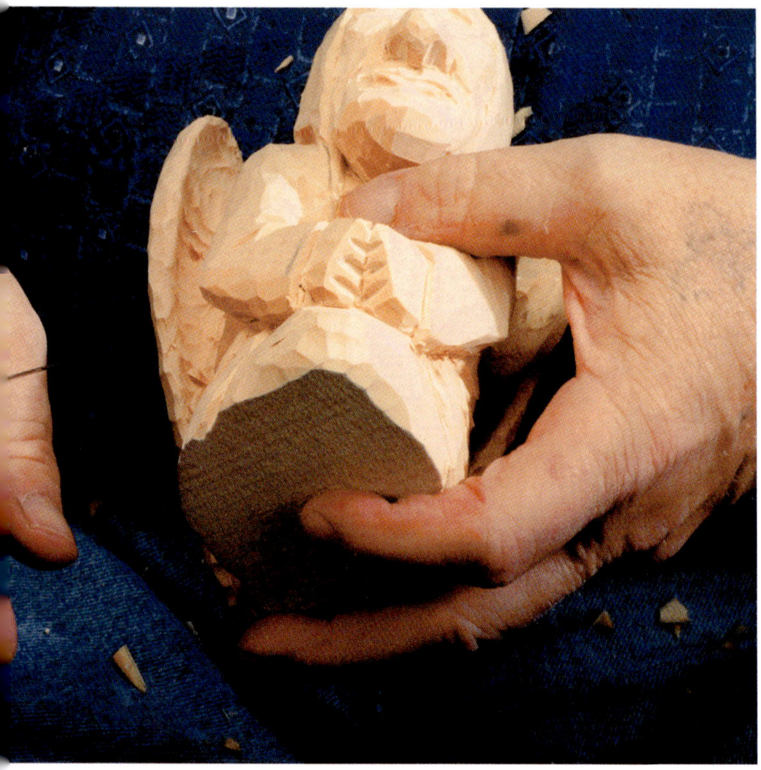

Progress.

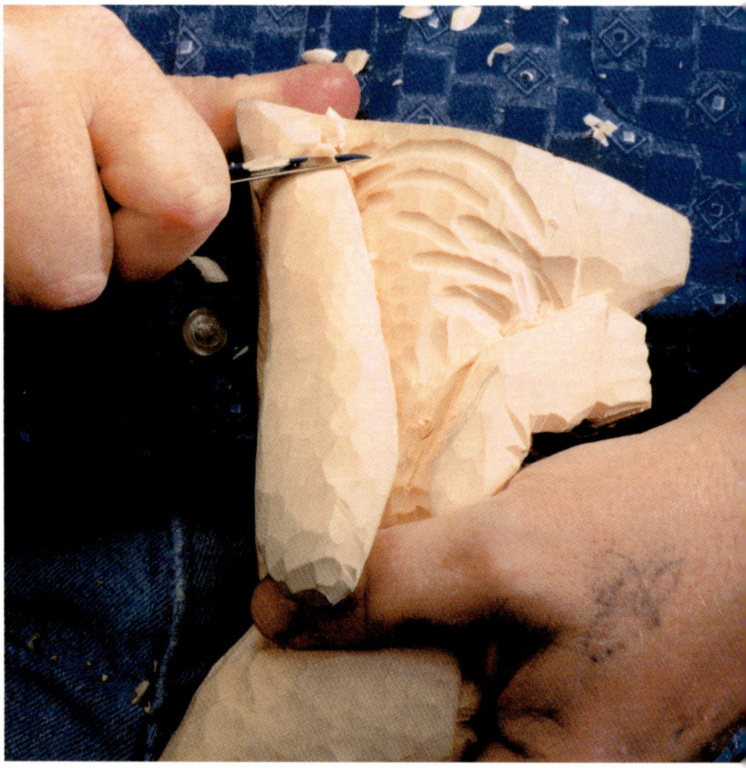

Now I'm going over the entire piece with the knife to get rid of any roughness or marks that don't belong.

Progress.

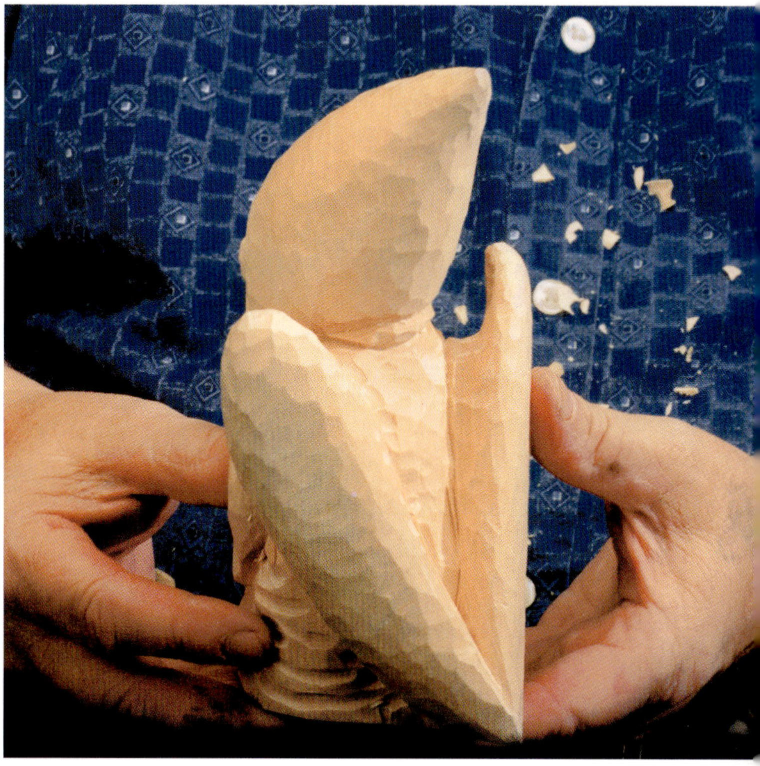

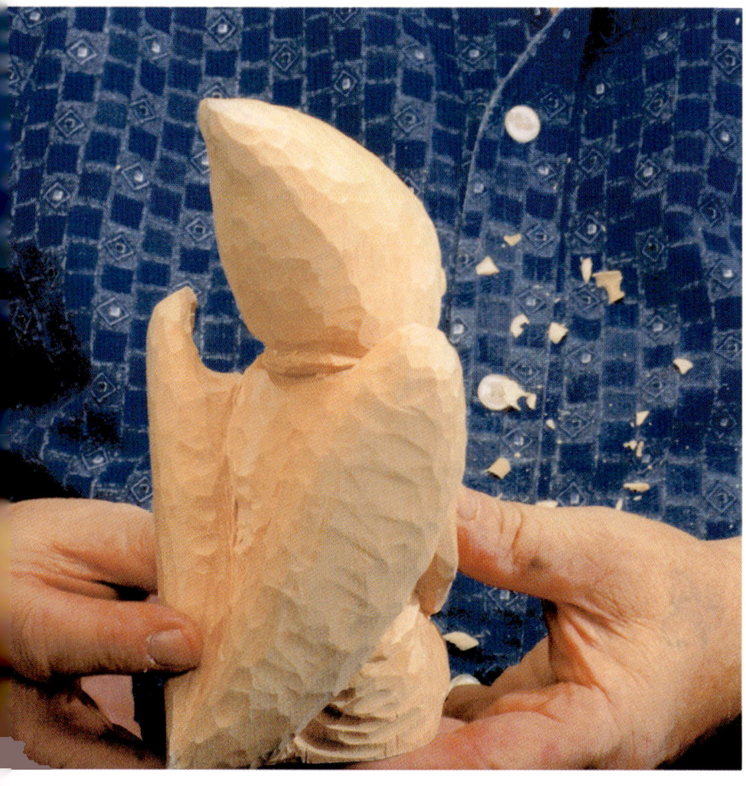

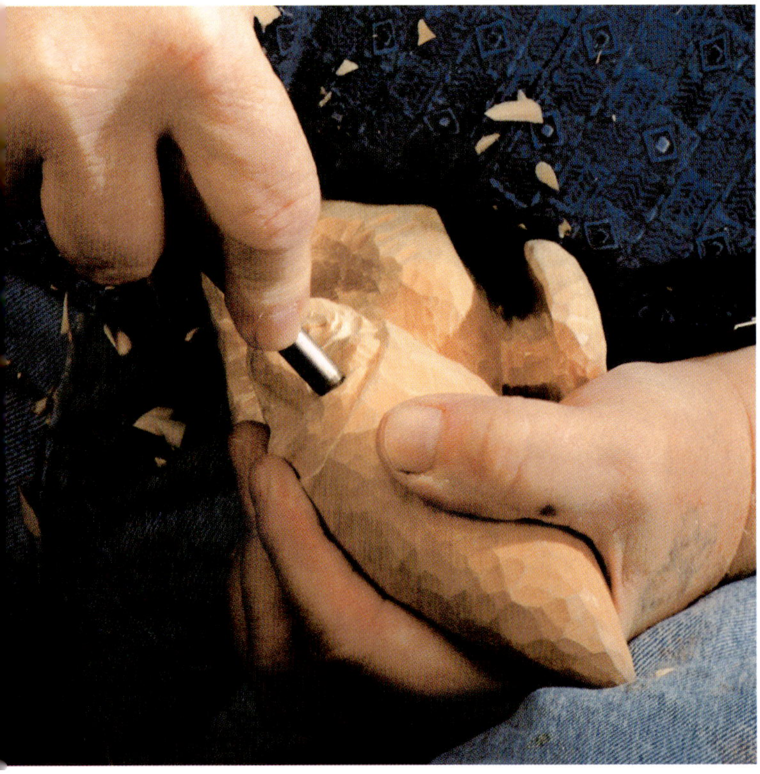

He needs some eyes. I have designed a set of eye punches that are available from Woodcraft—they make great eyes of all kinds for carvings. This one makes a half-circle. You simple determine where the eye belongs and push straight in, using a slight rocking motion.

I'm punching the other eye a little differently for a more interesting expression.

The half-circle gives him the appearance of looking up.

With the roundness of the eye established, the corners can be made using three tiny cuts on each side. The first and second cuts are stops, following the lines of the upper and lower eyelids. The third cut is made with the blade flat against the surface of the eyeball, and pushed into the triangle made by the other two cuts. Do one eye...

Make the eyelids by going around the edge of the eye with a veiner.

Then the other.

Progress.

A smaller eye punch forms the irises. Watch the placement of the irises when you're working with two differently shaped eyes. The irises should be in the same position in each eye.

The beard needs some texture. I'm using the veiner to make hair lines.

You can use the same tool to create the hair in the eyebrows. The finished beard and eyebrows.

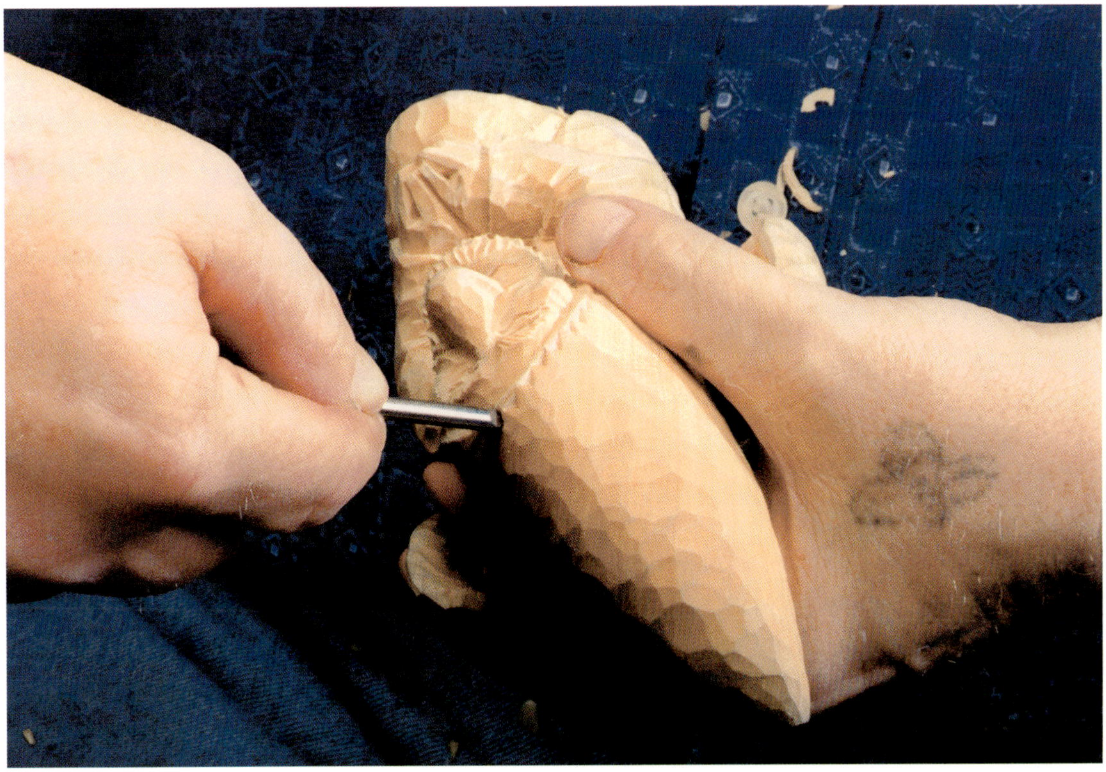

I call this tool the detail designer. I made it mysef by grinding a leather punch flat on one side and giving it two 45-degree bevels. It looks kind of like the nose of the stealth bomber! It's great to use for detail work and many different textures. He I'm using it to add some interest to the hem of the cloak.

Progress.

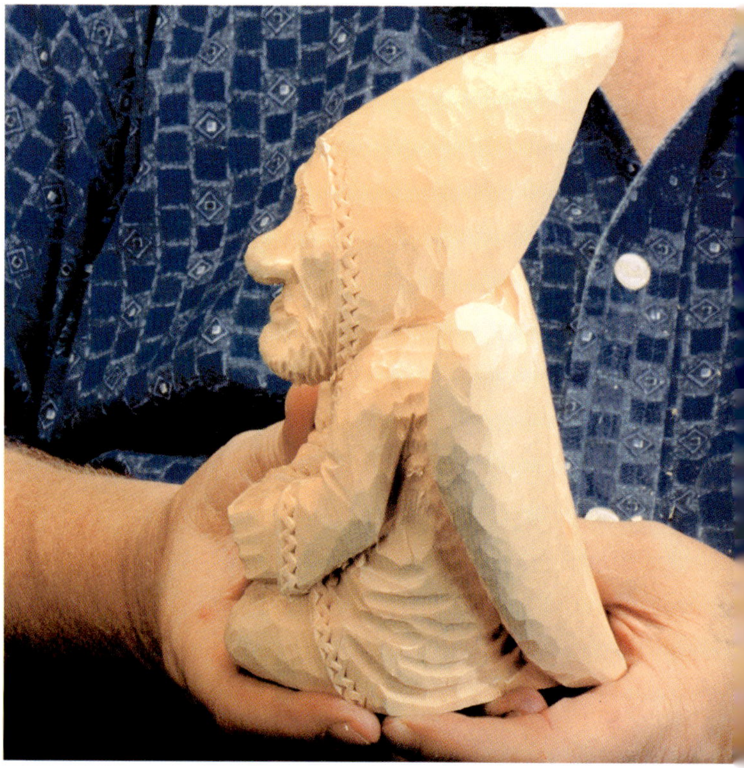

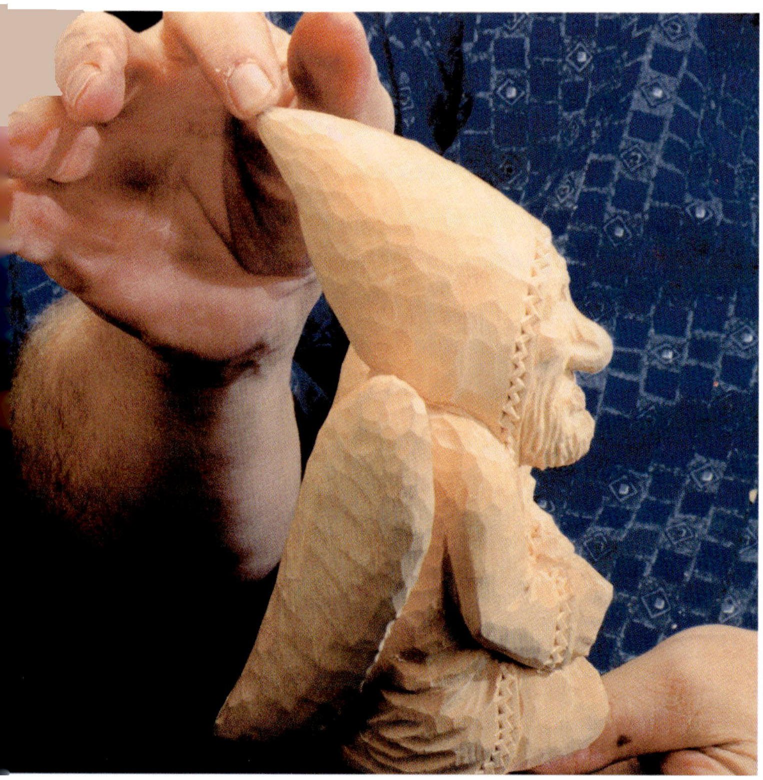

I think he should be wearing a tunic under the cloak. I'll use the detail designer for that too. First I'll carve the center line, using equally space notches from top to bottom.

Progress.

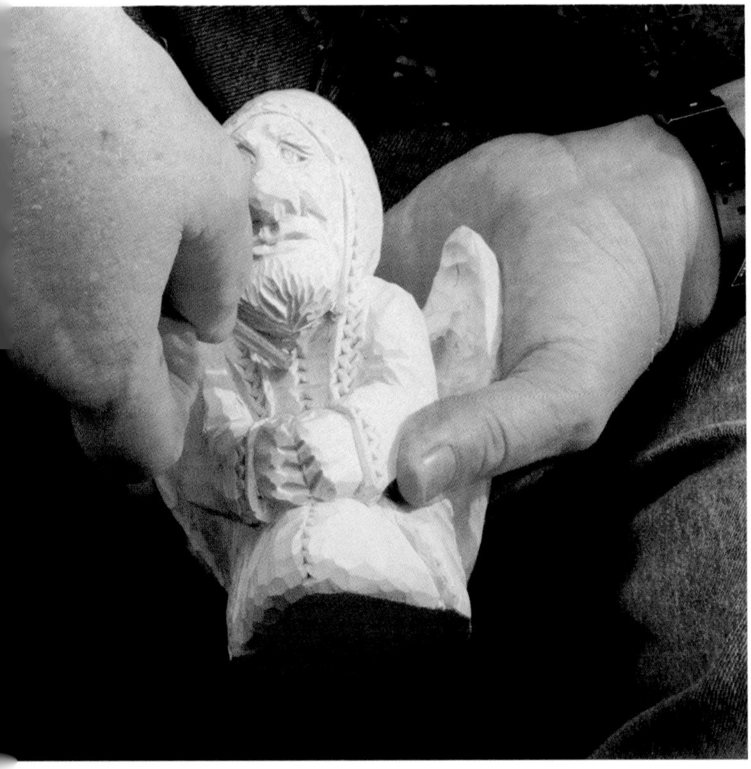

Turn the tool over so the triangles go the opposite way, and make a line of notches on both sides of the line.

Continue working out from the center, turning the tool for each row. The result is the woven look of this angel's tunic.

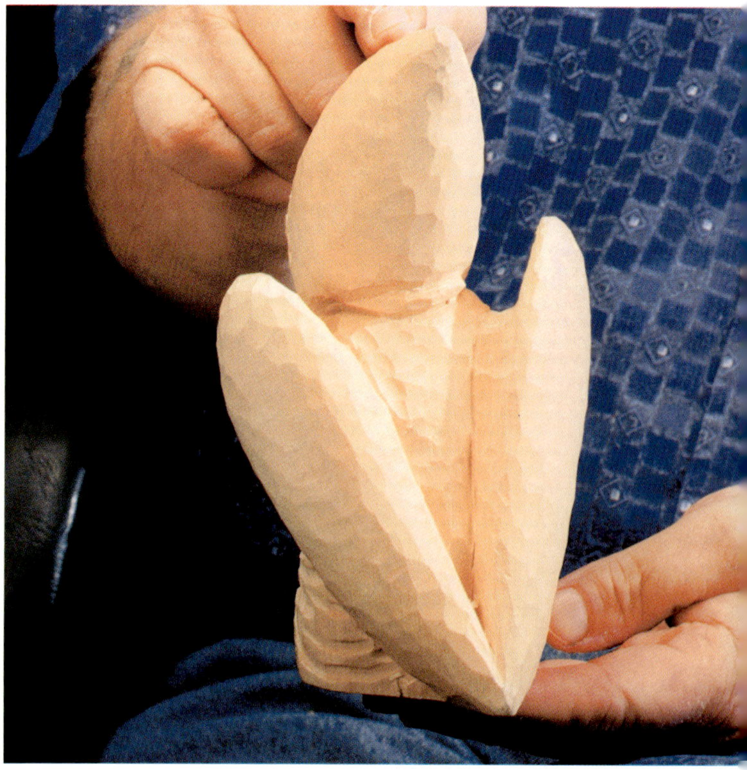

This finishes the carving and the angel is ready to paint.

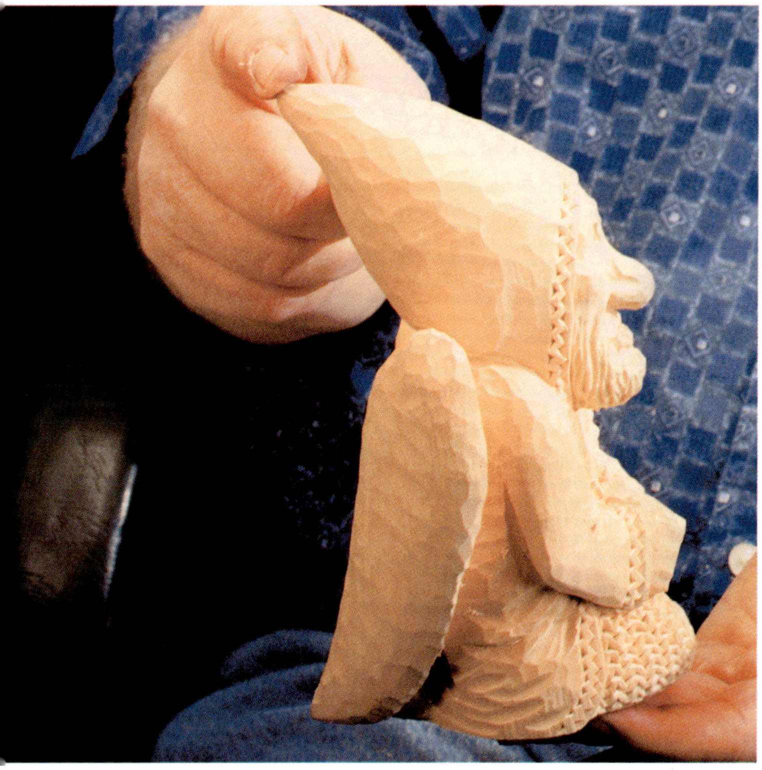

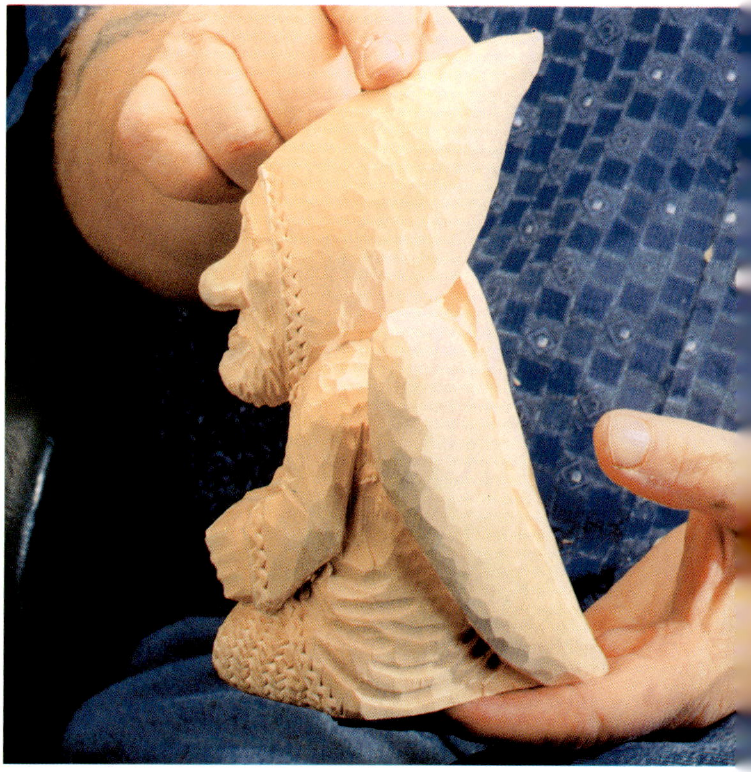

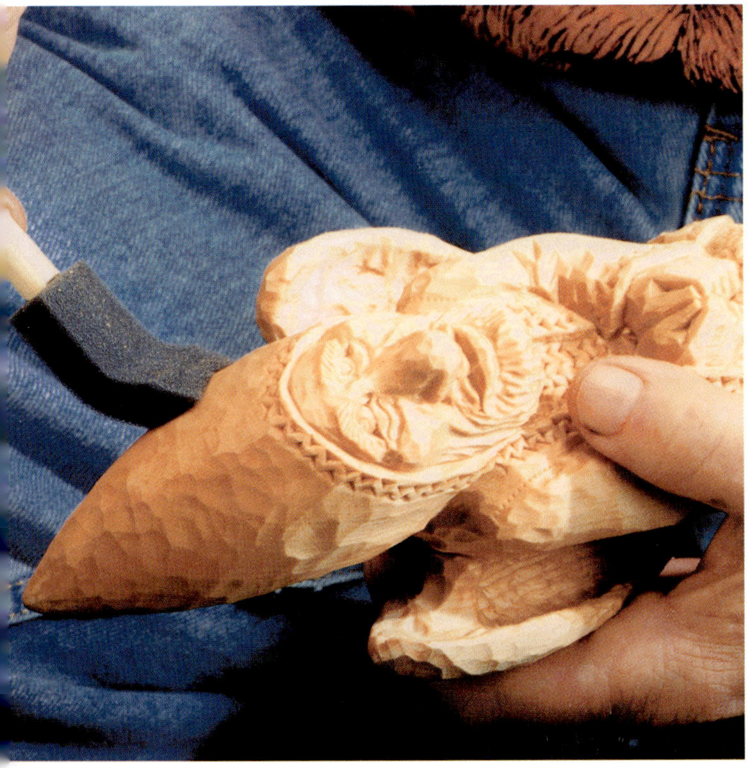

Before I paint, I like to brush on a coat of boiled linseed oil and let it dry overnight. If you can't wait, brush the linseed on and then blot off the excess with a paper towel.

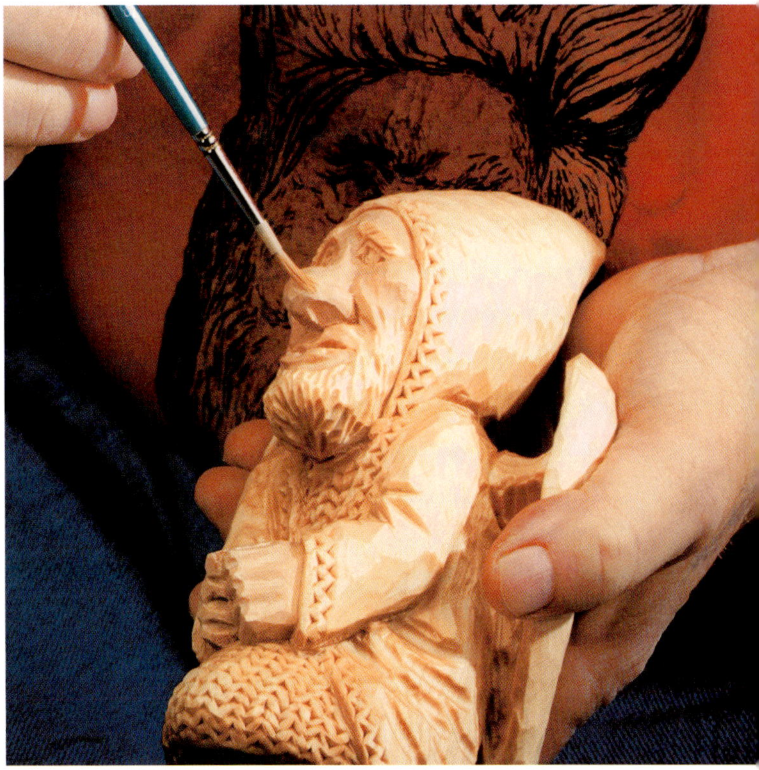

Brush on an even coat for the face.

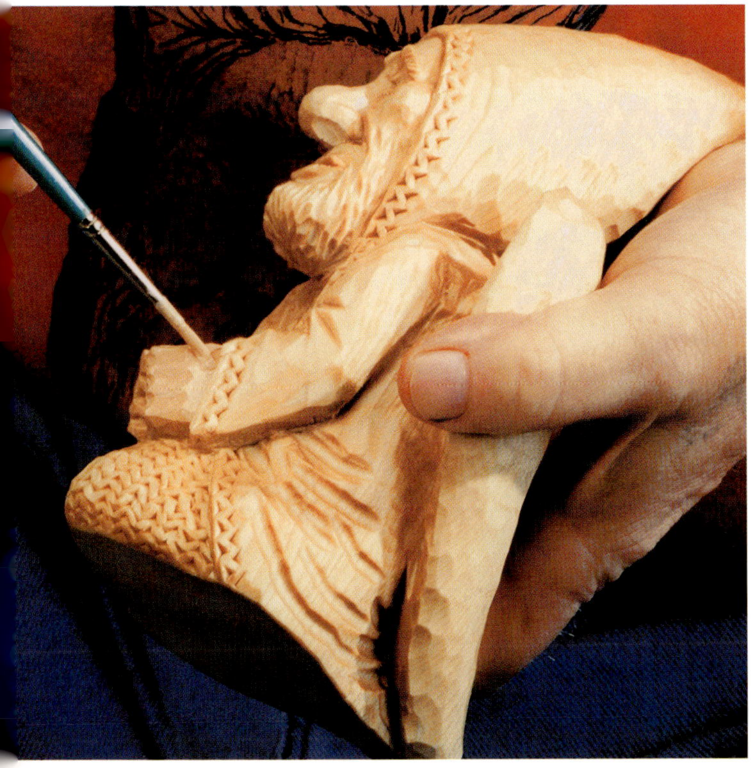

I start with the hands and face. My carvings are painted with artist's oils that I thin with turpentine so the grain of the wood still shows through. I make the flesh color by mixing a little flesh color out of the tube, a little raw sienna, and a lot of white. You'll probably need to experiment until you find a shade you like.

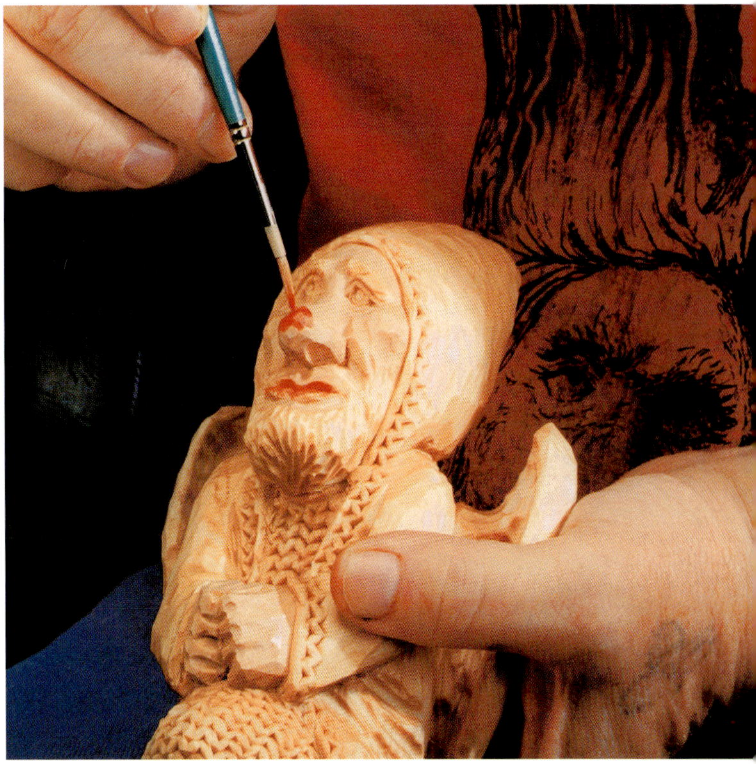

For the blush tones, dot some red on the lips, cheeks, nose, and even a little around the eyes...

then blend it in with a dry brush.

Progress. Make sure you brush out any puddles that may have gathered in the deeper cuts.

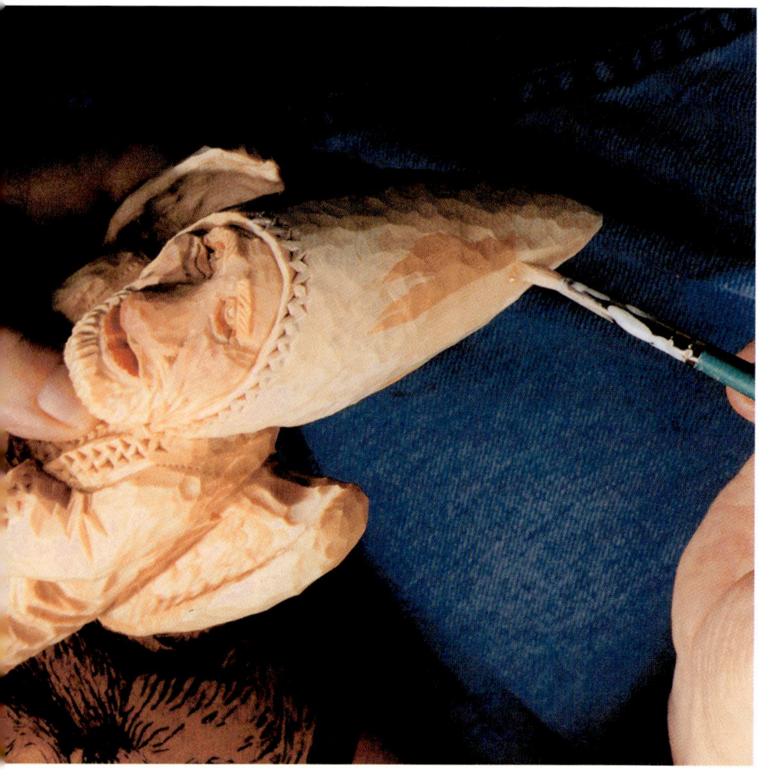

The cloak and hood for this angel will be white. I paint over the trim for now, but I'll come back later and highlight it with gold.

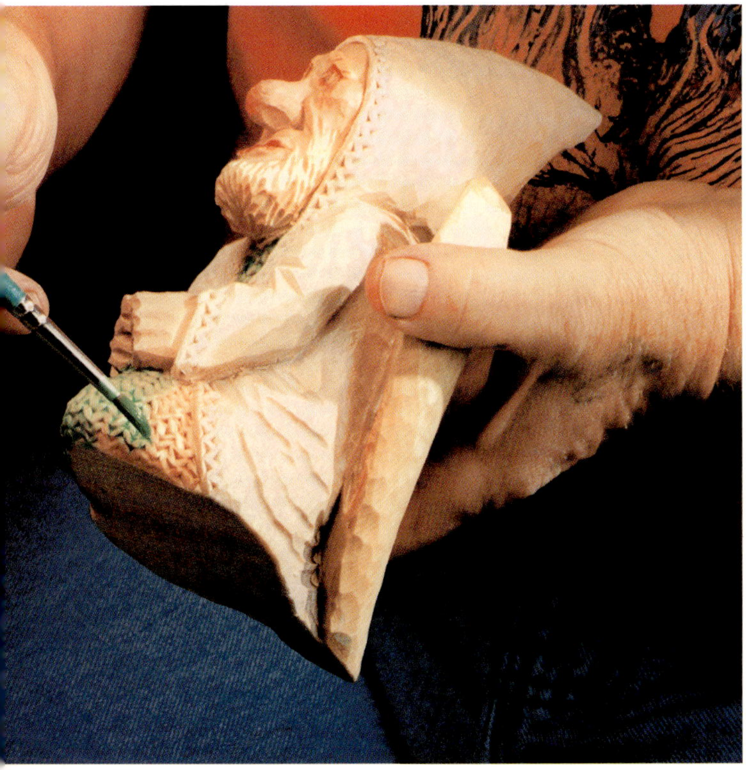

I'll make his tunic green. I'm putting the paint on pretty heavily so it flows into the punch marks.

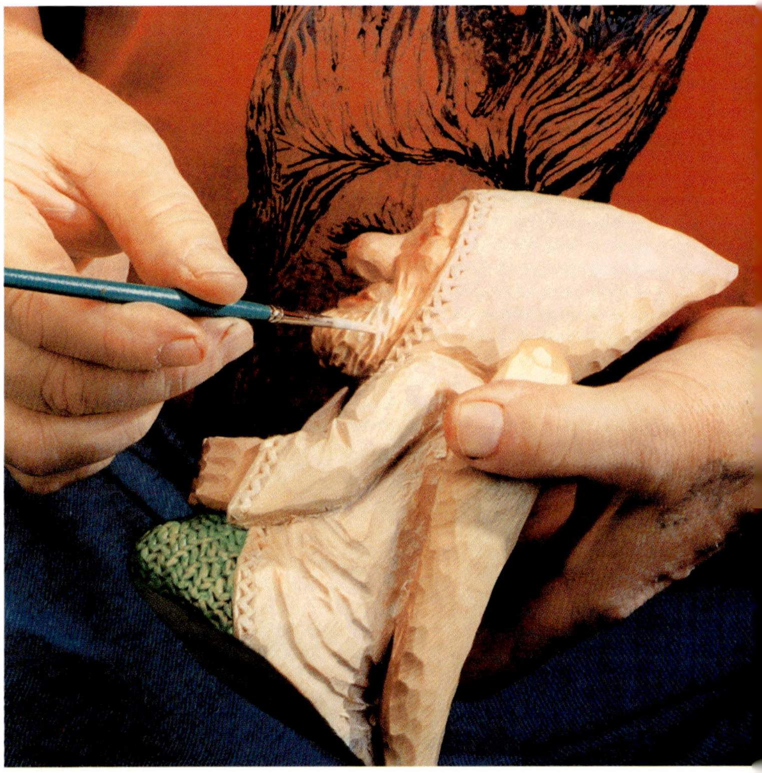

Brush a little white paint onto the beard.

Progress.

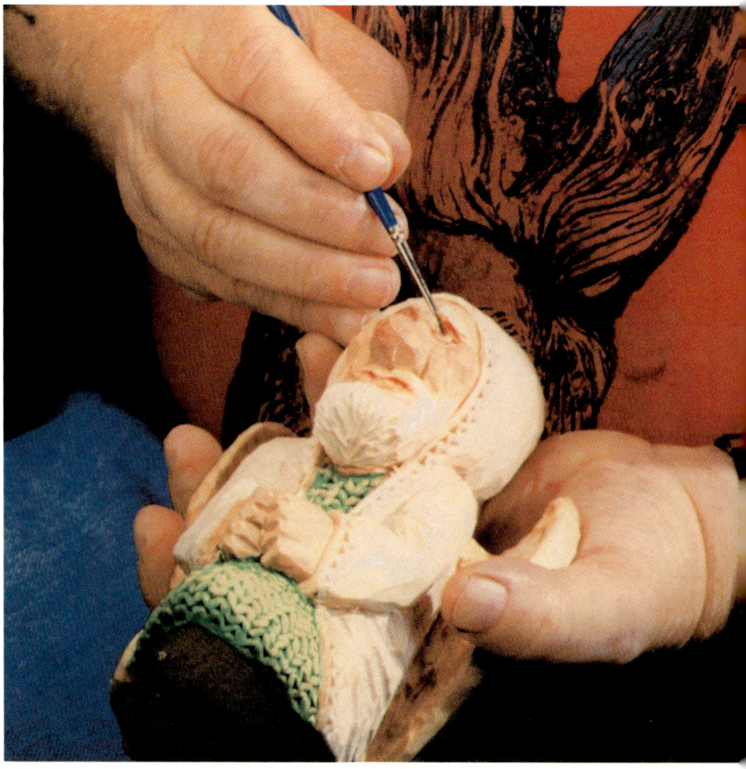

The irises are painted with a fine brush, using brown paint.

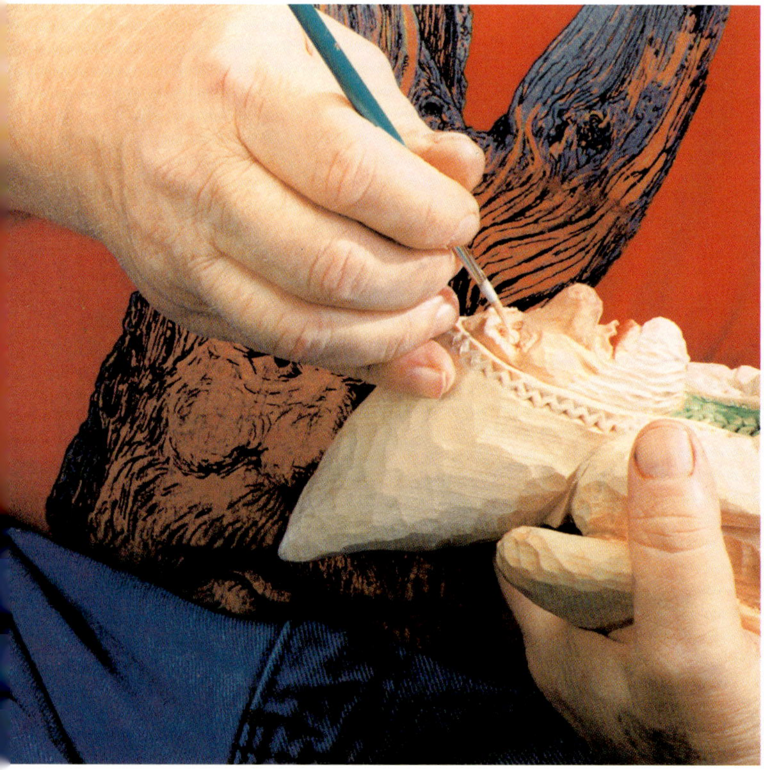

Dab some more white onto the eyebrows and the whites of the eyes.

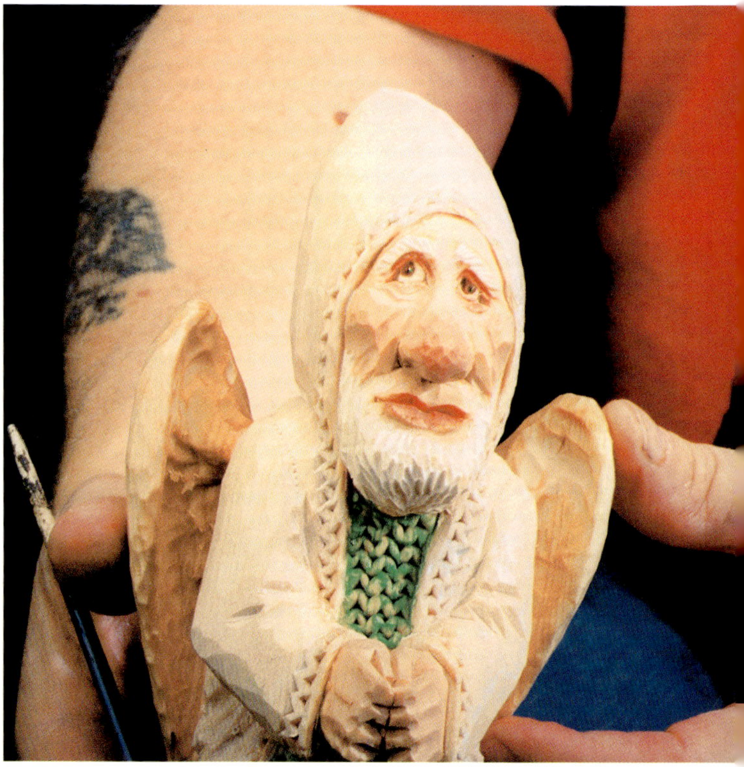

To give the eyes more interest and realism I added a little green dot and a little white dot to the irises.

A black permanent marker is good for dotting in the pupil. This is the result

Progress. Before adding the gold paint to the trim of the robe, I sprayed the carving with clear Deft to help set the paint and make it dry faster.

This gold metallic paint looks great on the wings.

Then, using the gold paint, I just trace the squiggly zig-zag I made with the Detail Designer.

The finished carving.

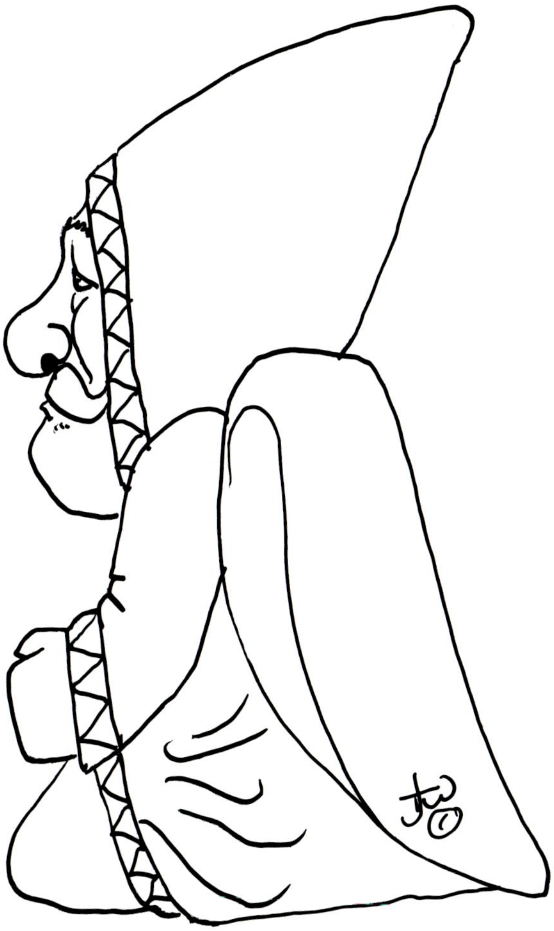

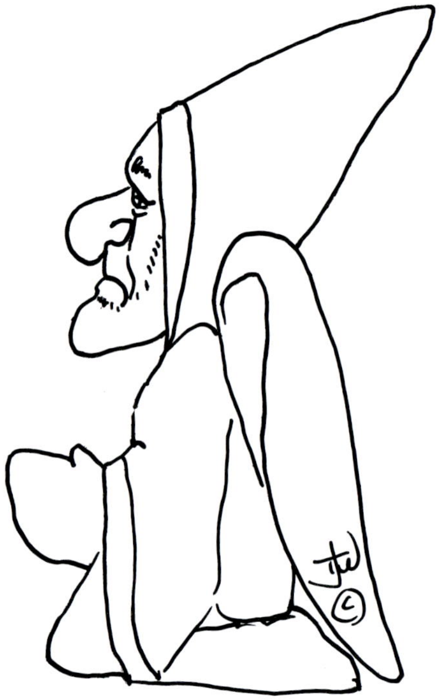